Ultrean Air Fryer Cookbook 2020-2021

800 Easy Tasty Air Fryer Recipes Cooked with Your Ultrean Air Fryer for Beginners and Advanced Users

By Dr. Mary Amanda

Table of Content

Foreward

In this comprehensive guide, we will introduce a multi-functional air fryer model and some of its unique functions that make it already stand out in the market. There is no doubt that Ultrean Air Fryer is an amazing appliance that allows you to cook crispy and delicious food with low-fat dining experience. When you research the product and explore its features, you are going to love this gadget for all the conveniences that it will bring to you.

In this one-stop guide, we will discuss:
- Basics of Ultrean Air Fryer
- Simple-to-Use Buttons and Functions
- Tips and Cautions of Usage
- Cleaning and Maintenance
- Cooking Timetable
- FAQs
- Easy tasty recipes

This book is for all food lovers who want to enjoy some crunchy and healthy recipes with less oil to maintain their healthy condition. With this cookbook, you can enjoy low-fat, healthy but scrumptious meals at any time without sacrificing the taste and texture of your food.

After using the Ultrean Air Fryer, you will realize this is definitely a product that you can trust. It is one of the highest reviewed and rated appliances on Amazon.com.

Introduction to Ultrean Air Fryer

The Ultrean fryer is a 4.2 quarter air fryer that allows everyone to deep fry their meals with less oil. Deep frying with this air fryer does not use oil at all. This air fryer is undoubtedly a much more effective and efficient appliance, with much less oil being used during cooking.

The Ultrean Air Fryer offers you the advantages of a versatile cookware that can be used for a variety of tasks. **You can deep fry as well as roast, bake, and grill your personal favorite meals with the help of Ultrean air fryer.** The Ultrean air fryer's versatility ensures a heating system known as fast technology. This innovative heating system is designed to cook meals evenly without the use of a thermometer or hot oil.

So, if you want more than just a standard air fryer, you should buy the Ultrean Air Fryer.

On top of that, it is very easy to use. The users can very easily set the appliance as well as the adjustable cooking time. The Ultrean air fryer is equipped with an automatic switch for setting the timer from 0 to 30 minutes. This means that if you forget to turn off the appliance, it will turn off automatically after the scheduled time. The automatic turn-off function will also be activated to ensure safety in certain cases where you turn on the appliance for more than 30 minutes without cooking. .The Ultrean Air Fryer has a temperature adjustment range between 180 degrees Fahrenheit and 400 degrees Fahrenheit.

It has been proved to be a versatile surprise when it comes to cooking various foods. You can also use this appliance to double fry your food and even heat it in the most authentic way.

The Ultrean Air Fryer also has some features which is similar to other air fryer products in the market. For example, this air fryer is very easy to maintain and clean, and it comes with a non-stick pan and heat-resistant handle to ensure safety and reduce the chances of burning yourself. It also has a removable basket. The contemporary design is very simple and classic with an LCD screen. An added feature of this appliance is that you also get a recipe book, showcasing some versatile food types such as fried food items, snacks and baking.

What Is It?

Everyone loves fried food and most people find themselves fascinated with the scrumptious taste from the fried food. However, what we all know is that too much oil consumption is not doing any good for your health. You might put your health in danger just by eating fried food twice a week.

It is hardly possible to say goodbye to fried food and that is how the air fryer is invented. The

Ultrean Air Fryer is an appliance which performs even better than many other brands and models in the market. With the Ultrean Air Fryer, you only need to put a very limited amount of oil and are able to get the same crunchy taste. Using oil spray or a splash of oil is all you need to cook a deliciously crunchy and healthy food.

The Ultrean Air Fryer circulates hot air around food place in the basket to crisp up the food. It works in the same way as a deep fryer. A plus point of the Ultrean is that you can turn it on to see the progress of your food without losing the heating effect or time.

Different personalized meals are made to the perfect level. It is truly miraculous that this appliance can be used for chicken wings, fried vegetables, and even for baking purposes. It has been tested that the Ultrean Air Fryer is able to make the food taste exactly the same as fast food with much less oil.

The Ultrean Air Fryer has a technology that offers some specific cooking methods to bake and to reheat food. The Ultrean Air Fryer's display is so easy to use that you will not need to read the instruction before using it.

Temperature and time can be adjusted manually.

You can adjust the temperature and set the time based on your preference. This is a multi-functional air fryer and it is the solution to all your cooking problems. The Ultrean Air Fryer is a very practical kitchen gadget that is a great alternative to any heavy-duty air fryer.

Simple-to-Use Buttons and Functions

- Rapid Air Technology
- Accessible Buttons
- Scratch Free Modern Design
- LCD
- Detachable Cooking Pot
- Adjustable Timer and Temperature

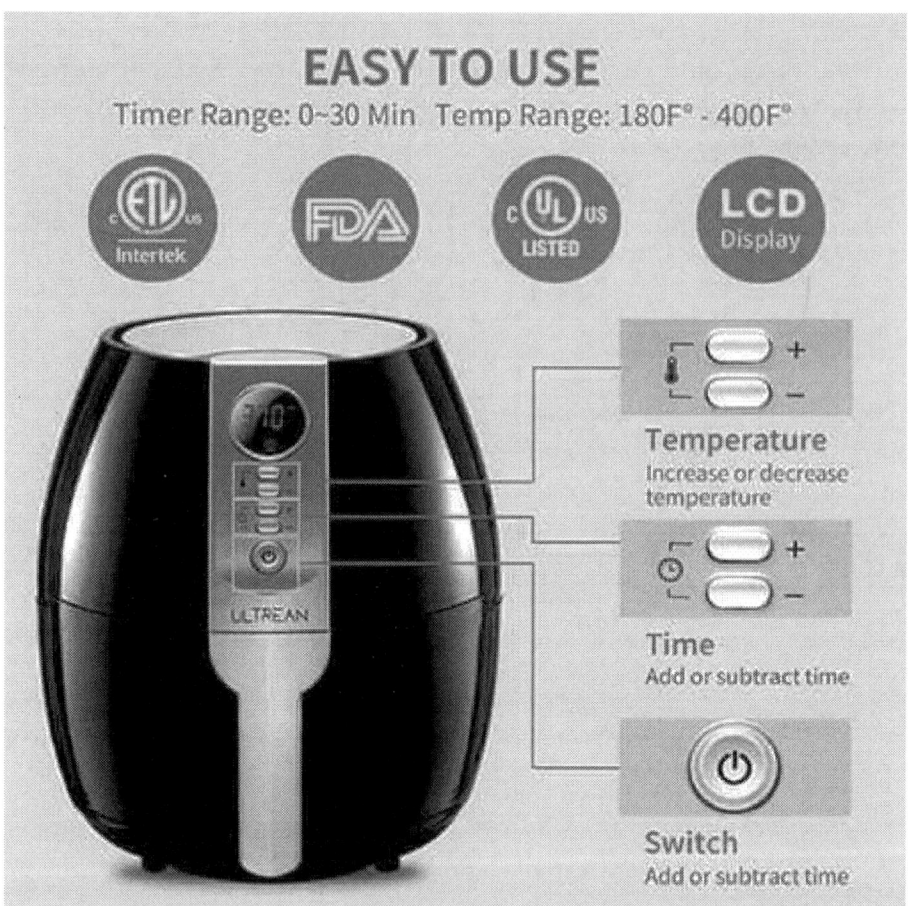

EASY TO USE

Timer Range: 0~30 Min   Temp Range: 180F° - 400F°

Temperature
Increase or decrease temperature

Time
Add or subtract time

Switch
Add or subtract time

Tips and Cautions of Usage

Listed below are some of the tips and cautions that should be considered while operating the appliance.

- Do not touch the appliance during the cooking process since the heat might be remained.
- Use oven glove while handling hot material or using the hard part of the appliance.
- Do not put anything on top of the appliance while it is on operational mode.
- Always remember to check the instruction manual before using the appliance.
- The cord of the appliance should be plugged into the right electrical outlet.
- Please do not try to repair it at home when the appliance is not malfunctioning.
- Do not leave the appliance unattended during the cooking process
- Do not emerge the power code of the air fly into any liquid.
- Set the air fryer on a flat and heat resistant working area
- Keep the air fryer 6 inches away from the wall and other objects around it.
- Check the air fryer basket to make sure that it is locked in the exact position in the drawer.
- The appliance is for household use so it should not be used inside the vehicle or outdoor.

- Unplug the appliance after use.
- Let the air cool down for 30 minutes before you handle or clean it.

Cleaning and Maintenance

First, unplug the power cord from the socket and let the appliance cool after cooking is complete.

Before cleaning make sure the appliance is cooled.

Now soak the accessories in warm soapy water to remove grease and dust.

Clean the basket of the air fryer with a soft sponge which is dipped in a mild detergent or use dishwasher to clean it.

You can put all of the parts in the dishwasher.

Remove the unwanted food residue from the outer surface with a damp cloth.

Cooking Timetable

- Seafood: 390-400 for 4 -12 minutes
- Vegetates: 400 Degrees for 5 minutes
- Fries: 400 degrees F for 14 minutes
- Red Meat: 370-400 degrees F 10-20 minutes
- Pork: 360-400 degrees-4minute-hours
- Chicken: 360-400 degrees for 12-22 minutes
- Shrimp: 400 degrees F for 9 minutes
- Burger: 370 degrees F for 6 minutes

FAQs

Q: Is Ultrean Air Fryer a good appliance?
A: The BestViews Review Ranking for this appliance is 8.8 out of 10, which is awesome. This is a quality appliance that everyone should have.

Q: Is Ultrean Air Fryer easy to clean?
A: Well, the accessories of Ultrean Air Fryer are dishwasher safe and most of the grease can be removed with a scouring pad.

Q: How many people this model of air fryer can this feed?
A: Almost 3-4 people probably.

Q: Is there any option to lower the button sounds?
A: No, it cannot be adjusted.

Q: Can consumers cook more the one thing in it?
A: Yes, if they want to.

Q: It is ok to use tinfoil with the air fryer?
A: Yes, you can use it.

Chapter 1: Breakfast Recipes

Blackberry Pancake

This pancake recipe is fluffy and made from scratch. It's also thick and very filling.
Prep time and cooking time: 10 minutes|
Serves: 2

Ingredients To Use:

- 1-1/2 cups almond flour
- Salt and pepper to taste
- 3 tbsp. butter
- 3 medium eggs
- 2 tsp. dried basil
- 2 cups blackberry, minced
- 2 tsp. dried parsley

Step-by-Step Directions to Cook It:

1. Preheat the Air Fryer to 250°F.
2. Stir all ingredients together in a small bowl.
3. Grease the pancake molds with butter and pour in the batter. Place it in the Air Fryer and cook on both sides till golden brown.
4. Serve with honey.

Nutritional value per serving:

Calories: 152kcal, Fat: 10g, Carb: 22g, Proteins: 5g

Tuna Sandwich

This jazzed-up tuna recipe melts right in your mouth. It's also hot and spicy, which makes it a perfect breakfast for a cold day.
Prep time and cooking time: 15 minutes|
Serves: 2

Ingredients To Use:

- 1 tin tuna
- 1 tbsp. softened butter
- 1 small capsicum, peeled, roasted, and sliced
- 2 slices of white bread

Sauce Ingredients:

- 1/4 cup chopped onion
- 1/2 cup of water
- 1/2 tsp. olive oil
- 1/4 tsp. mustard powder
- Salt and black pepper to taste
- 1 garlic clove, crushed
- 1/4 tbsp. red chili sauce
- 1/4 tbsp. Worcestershire sauce
- 1/2 tbsp. sugar
- 1 tbsp. tomato ketchup

Step-by-Step Directions to Cook It:

1. Cut out edges of the bread and then slice horizontally.
2. Cook sauce ingredients in a saucepan over medium heat. Add the tuna to the sauce and cook until fragrant.
3. Mix the capsicum with sauce and spread the mixture on bread slices.
4. Preheat the Air Fryer to 300°F for 5 minutes. Arrange the sandwich side by side into the Air Fryer basket. Cook both sides to a golden brown for about 15 minutes.
5. Serve.

Nutritional value per serving:

Calories: 102kcal, Fat: 8g, Carb: 4g, Proteins: 12g

Bread with Ham and Egg

This recipe is a cross between homemade French toast and ham sandwich, making you excited for the day.
Prep time and cooking time: 30 minutes|

Serves: 1

Ingredients To Use:

- 2 bread slices (brown or white)
- 1/2 lb. sliced ham, cooked
- 1 egg white
- 1 tsp. sugar

Step-by-Step Directions to Cook It:

1. Cut the bread slices diagonally.
2. Beat the egg whites and sugar in a small bowl.
3. Dip the bread into the egg mixture.
4. Preheat the Air Fryer to 350⁰F.
5. Transfer the coated slices into the Air Fryer basket and cook to golden brown on both sides.
6. Serve with slices of ham and cheese(optional)

Nutritional value per serving:

Calories: 232kcal, Fat: 25g, Carb: 28g, Proteins: 18g

Strawberry Tart

Tart filled fruits are very common in some countries like Morocco. The recipe is topped with colourful strawberries that make the tart stunning.
Prep time and cooking time: 30 minutes|
Serves: 2

Ingredients To Use:

- 2 tbsp. powdered sugar
- 1-1/2 cup of plain flour
- 3 tbsp. unsalted butter
- 2 cups cold water

Fillings:

- 1 cup fresh cream
- 3 tbsp. butter
- 2 cups sliced strawberries

Step-by-Step Directions to Cook It:

1. Combine all ingredients apart from fillings in a large bowl. Knead the dough with fresh cold milk and wrap it up with a plastic bag for about 10 minutes.
2. Stir in the filling ingredients in another bowl. Using a rolling pin, roll out the dough into pie and spoon the strawberry mixture in between. Press pie edges with a fork. Spray the tart with cooking spray.
3. Preheat the Air Fryer to 300⁰F for 5 minutes.
4. Transfer the tart to an Air Fryer basket. Cook to a golden brown and serve with candy sprinkles.

Nutritional value per serving:

Calories: 229kcal, Fat: 9g, Carb: 39g, Proteins: 2g

Almond Milk

The recipe is a creamy, custardy dessert that has a soft texture. It melts when it hits your tongue and can be served with strawberries or dried fruit.
Prep time and cooking time: 10minutes |
Serves: 4

Ingredients To Use:

- 1 tsp. gelatin
- 2 tbsp. custard powder
- 3 tbsp. powdered sugar
- 2 cups almond powder
- 2 cups of milk

Step-by-Step Directions to Cook It:

1. Heat the milk and sugar in a saucepan over medium heat. Thicken the mixture with almond powder, custard powder, and gelatin.
2. Preheat the Air Fryer to 300⁰F.
3. Place the saucepan containing the milk mixture into the Air Fryer.

4. Cook for about 10 minutes and then allow to cool.

Nutritional value per serving:
Calories: 148kcal, Fat: 1.6g, Carb: 28.8g, Proteins: 4.7g

Honey Glazed Donut

This is just the first of many awesome doughnut recipes you will come across in this book. Doughnuts are delicious, soft, and lip-smacking, and this particular recipe requires simple ingredients that can be easily available on your pantry.
Prep time and cooking time: 25 minutes|
Serves: 8

Ingredients To Use:
- 1-1/2 cups powdered sugar
- 2 tsp. honey
- 2 tbsp. milk
- 1 can large flaky-style biscuit dough
- 1/4 cup butter, melted

Step-by-Step Directions to Cook It:
1. Cut out the dough into eight biscuits. Make a hole in the middle of the biscuits using a round cutter. Brush butter on both sides of the biscuits and place them on a parchment or cookie sheet.
2. Place the biscuits in a preheated Air Fryer and bake at 330⁰F for 12 minutes.
3. Transfer the donuts to a cooling rack and allow to cool.
4. In a large-sized bowl, combine honey and powdered sugar. Add milk until the desired consistency is reached. Dunk donuts in the honey mixture.
5. Serve.

Nutritional value per serving:
Calories: 207kcal, Fat: 7g, Carb: 31g, Proteins: 3g

Baked Eggs in Brioche

This classic recipe consists of a perfectly baked egg nestled in the middle of a French bread. It's soft and tasty.
Prep time and cooking time: 15 minutes|
Serves: 3

Ingredients To Use:
- 3 slices cheddar cheese
- 3 medium eggs
- 1 tbsp. chives
- 3 brioche rolls (about 3 × 3 inches in size)
- 3 tbsp. butter, melted
- Salt and pepper, to taste

Step-by-Step Directions to Cook It:
1. Remove the top of the brioche (1 inch) to make a hole using a round cutter. Brush the edges with butter and place cheese inside the brioche.
2. Crack one egg into each brioche and sprinkle in salt, chives, and pepper.
3. Arrange the brioche into the Air Fryer basket and bake for 10 minutes at 330⁰F.
4. Serve.

Nutritional value per serving:
Calories: 140kcal, Fat: 7g, Carb: 15g, Proteins: 3g

Air Fried Creamy Hash Brown Casserole

This easy cheesy breakfast recipe will wholly satisfy you. The casserole is filled with creamy and tasty ingredients.
Prep time and cooking time: 30 minutes|
Serves: 2

Ingredients To Use:
- 1 cup shredded cheddar cheese
- 1/2 cup breadcrumbs
- 2 tbsp. butter, melted

- 10.5 oz. chicken soup
- 1/2 cup sour cream
- 1/2 tsp. salt
- 1-1/2 cups shredded hash brown potatoes
- 1/3 cup chopped onion

Step-by-Step Directions to Cook It:

1. In a large bowl, combine the cream and soup. Season with salt. Add the onions, hash brown, and cheese. Spoon the mixture into a baking dish and set aside.
2. In another bowl, combine the breadcrumbs and butter. Add the bread mixture evenly into the baking dish.
3. Place the dish into the preheated Air Fryer and bake at 300⁰F for 15 minutes.
4. Serve when cool.

Nutritional value per serving:

Calories: 280kcal, Fat: 20g, Carb: 15g, Proteins: 5g

Greek Feta Baked Omelette

The Greek feta omelette is loaded with Greek flavors that are irresistible. Get the eggs cracking!
Prep time and cooking time: 10 minutes | Serve: 2

Ingredients To Use:

- 1/8 tsp. oregano
- 3 eggs, lightly beaten
- 6 cherry tomatoes, quartered
- 3 tbsp. frozen leaf spinach, thawed and drained
- 2 tbsp. crumbled feta cheese

Step-by-Step Directions to Cook It:

1. Coat the inside of a baking dish with cooking oil. Stir in eggs and add cheese, spinach, and oregano.
2. Place the dish into a preheated Air Fryer.

3. Bake at 330⁰F for 6 minutes.

Nutritional value per serving:

Calories: 207kcal, Fat: 14g, Carb: 6g, Proteins: 16g

Air Fried Garlic Bacon and Potatoes

The golden-brown air-fried potatoes are baked with bacon to make delicious and crispy bites.
Prep time and cooking time: 30 minutes| Serve: 4

Ingredients To Use:

- 2 sprigs of rosemary
- 4 medium-sized Yukon Gold potatoes, peeled and cut into halves
- 4 strips of streaky bacon
- 6 cloves of garlic, smashed
- 3 tsp. vegetable oil

Step-by-Step Directions to Cook It:

1. Preheat the Air Fryer to 390°F.
2. Mix all the ingredients in a large bowl.
3. Roast them in an Air Fryer basket for 25 minutes.
4. Serve.

Nutritional value per serving:

Calories: 226kcal, Fat: 12g, Carb: 28g, Proteins: 10g

Air Fried Sausage

The Air Fryer makes the golden-brown sausage patties by using no stovetop oil. So you don't have to worry about the oil splatter.
Prep time and cooking time: 20 minutes| Serves: 6

Ingredients To Use:

- 1 tsp. salt

- 1 tsp. paprika
- 1 tsp. dried thyme
- 2 tsp. fennel seed
- 1 tsp. maple syrup
- 2 lbs. ground turkey
- 2 tsp. dry rubbed sage

Step-by-Step Directions to Cook It:

1. Combine all ingredients in a large size bowl.
2. Spoon the mixture into a ball, and then make patties using your palm.
3. Place the patties into the Air Fryer basket.
4. Cook at 350⁰F for about 10 minutes. Cook in batches if necessary.
5. Serve.

Nutritional value per serving:

Calories: 170kcal, Fat: 15g, Carb: 10g, Proteins: 6g

Crunchy carrot

Air fried carrot can be added to your breakfast menu, especially if you are a big fan of veggies. Enjoy with honey or maple syrup.
Prep time and cooking time: 22 minutes| Serves: 2

Ingredients To Use:

- 4 carrots, sliced horizontally
- 1 tbsp. olive oil
- Salt to taste

Step-by-Step Directions to Cook It:

1. Coat the carrot with olive oil and season with salt.
2. Preheat the Air Fryer to 360⁰F
3. Cook the carrot until tender.
4. Serve.

Nutritional value per serving:

Calories: 22kcal, Fat: 3g, Carb: 0g, Proteins: 0g

Grilled Cheese

It's super easy to create a crispy delight by spreading the cheese and butter mixture on a toasted bread.
Prep time and cooking time: 15 minutes| Serves: 2

Ingredients To Use:

- 1/2 cup cheddar cheese
- 4 slices white bread
- 1/4 cup butter softened

Step-by-Step Directions to Cook It:

1. Preheat the Air Fryer to 360°F.
2. Spread the butter on each bread.
3. Cover each bread with another slice. Stuff cheese in between the bread slices and place them into the Air Fryer.
4. Cook for about 5 minutes to a golden brown.

Nutritional value per serving:

Calories: 490kcal, Fat: 23g, Carb: 14g, Proteins: 0g

Mini Sausage Roll

Sausage is rolled in flatbread before air fried to golden brown. The good part about this recipe is that it can be served at parties.
Prep time and cooking time: 20 minutes| Serves: 4

Ingredients To Use:

- 1 packet of flatbread
- 10 mini beef sausage

Step-by-Step Directions to Cook It:

1. Slice the bread into triangles. Roll each sausage in the triangular bread until all are well wrapped.
2. Preheats our Air Fryer to 356°F and

place the rolls in the fryer basket. Bake them for 15 minutes until crispy, and flip the rolls in between the cooking.

Nutritional value per serving:

Calories: 182kcal, Fat: 12 g, Carb: 8g, Proteins: 6g

Air Fryer Bacon and Egg

This recipe is a total bomb! It's easy to make and cheesy on the inside. The best part is that it requires few ingredients.
Prep time and cooking time: 50 minutes | Serves: 8

Ingredients To Use:

- 1/4 tsp. pepper
- 1 can buttermilk biscuits (5 biscuits)
- 2 oz. cheddar cheese, cut into cubes
- 4 slices bacon, cut into 1/2-inch pieces, cooked to crispy
- 1 tbsp. butter
- 2 eggs, beaten and fried
- 1 egg

Step-by-Step Directions to Cook It:

1. Use a cutter to cut around a parchment paper to make it fit the Air Fryer. Place it in the Air Fryer and spray with cooking oil.
2. Cut out dough into five biscuits and further cut each biscuit into two layers. Spoon the egg and bacon into the center and pinch edges to seal.
3. Mix one egg and water in a small bowl. Coat the biscuit with egg wash using a brush.
4. Place the biscuits in the Air Fryer.
5. Set to 325^{0}F and cook for 10 minutes.
6. Cook for a longer time if necessary.

Nutritional value per serving:

Calories: 200kcal, Fat: 12g, Carb: 17g, Proteins: 7g

Hard-Boiled Egg

You can get a well-done hardboiled egg ready with an Air Fryer. It requires little energy and also saves water. Superb!
Prep time and cooking time: 20 minutes| Serves: 6

Ingredients To Use:

- 6 large eggs

Step-by-Step Directions to Cook It:

1. Preheat the Air Fryer to 270^{0}F.
2. Carefully place the eggs in the Air Fryer and cook for 15 minutes.

Nutritional value per serving:

Calories: 77kcal, Fat: 5g, Carb: 0.5g, Proteins: 3g

Soft Boiled Egg

Low carbs and very easy to cook. Soft boiled eggs can be enjoyed with varieties of the other air-fried recipes in this book, such as Almond Milk and Air Fried Sausage.
Prep time and cooking time: 20 minutes| Serves: 4

Ingredients To Use:

- 4 large eggs

Step-by-Step Directions to Cook It:

1. Preheat the Air Fryer to 270^{0}F.
2. Carefully place the eggs in the Air Fryer and cook for 10 minutes.
3. Allow to cool and enjoy.

Nutritional value per serving:

Calories: 70kcal, Fat: 4g, Carb: 0.5g, Proteins: 4g

Breakfast Potatoes

Air fried breakfast potatoes are loaded with ingredients ranging from bell pepper to

onions, potatoes, and cloves. It's worth a try.
Prep time and cooking time: 30 minutes|
Serves: 4

- 1 tbsp. olive oil
- 1/4 tsp. pepper
- 1/2 tsp. salt
- 1/2 tsp. paprika
- 1-1/2 lbs. potatoes, diced and sakes in water
- 1/4 onion (chopped)
- 1 green bell pepper, washed chopped, and soaked in water.
- 2 garlic cloves (minced)

Step-by-Step Directions to Cook It:

1. Combine all ingredients in a bowl and place them in the Air Fryer basket.
2. Cook in the Air Fryer at 350⁰F for 25 minutes. Shake the basket at a 10 minutes interval till it completely cooked. Serve.

Nutritional value per serving:

Calories: 153kcal, Fat: 15g, Carb: 18g, Proteins: 3g

Toast Sticks

There are different ways to make a French toast recipe by using an Air Fryer. In this recipe, you get to try one of those methods.
Prep time and cooking time: 40 minutes|
Serves: 6

Ingredients To Use:

- 2 large eggs
- Kosher salt
- 6 thick slices Pullman, sliced into thirds
- Honey or maple syrup, for serving
- 1/3 cup of heavy cream
- 1/3 cup of whole milk
- 3 tbsp. granulated sugar

- 1/4 tsp. ground cinnamon
- 1/2 tsp. pure vanilla extract

Step-by-Step Directions to Cook It:

1. Whisk all ingredients in a bowl except for the Pullman slices.
2. Dunk in the slices and arrange in an Air Fryer basket.
3. Cook in the Air Fryer at 375⁰F for 8 minutes.
4. Serve with honey or maple syrup.

Nutritional value per serving:

Calories: 192kcal, Fat: 15g, Carb: 10g, Proteins: 8g

Air Fried Mozzarella Sticks

The homemade mozzarella cheese is healthier than the store-bought, and the best part is that all the ingredients can be gotten in the pantry and fridge.
Prep time and cooking time: 55 minutes|
Serves: 6

Ingredients To Use:

- 12 oz. package mozzarella cheese sticks, cut into halves
- 1/4 cup mayonnaise
- 1/2 tsp. garlic powder
- 1 large egg
- 1/4 cup all-purpose flour
- 1/4 cup fine, dry breadcrumbs
- 1/2 tsp. onion powder

Step-by-Step Directions to Cook It:

1. Freeze the cheese sticks for 30 minutes.
2. Beat the egg and mayonnaise in a bowl. Add the onions, breadcrumbs, onion, and garlic powder.
3. Dip the mozzarella sticks in the egg mixture and then in the flour mixture. Place them in the Air Fryer and cook for 5 minutes at 370⁰F.

4. Cook in batches if necessary
5. Serve with sauce.

Nutritional value per serving:
Calories: 232kcal, Fat: 20g, Carb: 10g, Proteins: 6g

Air Fried Beignets

There's so much more you can make with an Air Fryer, and beignet is one of them. Pull out your Air Fryer and start cooking.
Prep time and cooking time: 20 minutes|
Serves: 4

Ingredients To Use:
- 1-1/2 tsp. melted butter
- 1/2 tsp. baking powder
- 1/2 tsp. vanilla extract
- 1 pinch salt
- 2 tbsp. confectioners' sugar
- cooking spray
- 1/2 cup all-purpose flour
- 1/4 cup white sugar
- 1/8 cup of water
- 1 large egg, separated

Step-by-Step Directions to Cook It:
1. Preheat the Air Fryer to 370⁰F.
2. Using a cooking spray to grease the silicon egg mold.
3. Combine all ingredients except the egg white.
4. Use an electric mixer to mix the egg white until soft peaks are formed. Fold into batter.
5. Fill the mixture in a silicon mold and then place it into the Air Fryer.
6. Cook for 10 minutes and remove it from the mold.
7. Place it on a parchment sheet and replace it into the Air Fryer. Cook for

another 4 minutes. Sprinkle sugar on the beignets and serve.

Nutritional value per serving:
Calories: 88kcal, Fat: 1.7g, Carb: 16g, Proteins: 1.8g

Air Fried Caramelized Banana

This gooey snack can be served with a cup of warm milk. It's also very healthy and customizable.
Prep time and cooking time: 7 minutes|
Serves: 1

Ingredients To Use:
- 1 tbsp. coconut sugar
- Yogurt as toppings
- 2 bananas, peel and slice lengthwise
- 1/4 lemon, juiced

Step-by-Step Directions to Cook It:
1. Drizzle the lemon juice and sprinkle sugar atop banana.
2. Place the banana on a round parchment paper and put it into an Air Fryer.
3. Cook for 8 minutes at 400⁰F.
4. Top with yogurt.

Nutritional value per serving:
Calories: 60kcal, Fat: 10g, Carb: 6g, Proteins: 10g

Donut Sticks

This customized sugar-coated donut recipe is cooked in the Air Fryer, and best served warm.
Prep time and cooking time: 35 minutes|
Serves: 8

Ingredients To Use:
- 1 oz. refrigerated roll dough, cut into 1/2

inch lengthwise
- 1/2 cup sugar
- 1/2 cup flavored fruit jam
- 2 tsp. ground cinnamon
- 1/4 cup butter, melted

Step-by-Step Directions to Cook It:

1. Dunk the donut sticks in butter and arrange in an Air Fryer basket.
2. Set the Air Fryer to 380⁰F and cook the sticks for about 5 minutes.
3. Combine the cinnamon and sugar in a small bowl. Coat the air-fried donut in the cinnamon mixture.

Nutritional value per serving:

Calories: 266kcal, Fat: 11.8g, Carb: 37.6g, Proteins: 2.2g

Stuffed Bell Pepper

To start your day with a low carb meal rich in protein, try out the tenderly cooked stuffed bell pepper.
Prep time and cooking time: 20 minutes| Serves: 2

Ingredients To Use:

- 1 tsp. olive oil
- 4 eggs
- Salt and pepper to taste
- 1 bell pepper, halved and seeded

Step-by-Step Directions to Cook It:

1. Brush oil on bell pepper edges.
2. Crack two eggs into the bell pepper with the sunny side facing up. Season with salt and pepper.
3. Arrange the bell pepper into the Air Fryer basket.
4. Set the Air Fryer to 390F and cook for 13 minutes.
5. Serve.

Nutritional value per serving:

Calories: 164kcal, Fat: 10g, Carb: 4g, Proteins: 11g

Parmesan Baked Eggs

Air fried parmesan baked eggs make a tasty breakfast, and it's also time-saving when cooked in ramekins.
Prep time and cooking time: 10 minutes| Serves: 3

Ingredients To Use:

- 6 medium eggs
- 3 tbsp. Parmesan cheese, grated
- 3 tbsp. butter
- 1 shallot, minced
- 6 tsp. heavy cream
- 1 tbsp. minced fresh rosemary
- 1/2 tbsp. minced fresh thyme
- Salt and pepper, to taste

Step-by-Step Directions to Cook It:

1. Evenly divide the butter, thyme, rosemary, and shallot into three small ramekins.
2. Preheat the Air Fryer to 350⁰F.
3. Transfer the ramekins to an Air Fryer basket and cook for about 2 minutes, until the butter melts.
4. Carefully move out from the Air Fryer basket. Add cream and egg into the ramekins. Sprinkle in cheese atop the eggs and bake for 10 minutes.
5. Remove the ramekins from the oven and allow to cool before serving. Sprinkle in salt and pepper.

Nutritional value per serving:

Calories: 165kcal, Fat: 28g, Carb: 12g, Proteins: 10g

Chapter 2: Poultry Recipes

Buffalo Chicken Bowl

It's easy to throw together a chicken bowl It's loaded with veggies and also topped with irresistible tangy blue cheese.
Prep time and cooking time: 20 minutes | Serves: 4

Ingredients To Use:
- Blue cheese, for topping
- 2 tbsp. wing sauce
- 6 oz. cooked chicken breasts, diced
- 1-1/2 oz. blue cheese, crumbled
- 12 wonton wrappers
- 1/4 cup softened cream cheese
- 2 tbsp. ranch salad dressing

Step-by-Step Directions to Cook It:
1. In a medium-sized bowl, combine the hot wing sauce, softened cream cheese, chicken cheese, and ranch dressing.
2. Line the inside of the mini muffin pan with a piece of wonton wrapper each.
3. Fill each pan with the chicken mixture and ensure it doesn't get filled to the top.
4. Set the Air Fryer to 330⁰F.
5. Place the pan in the Air Fryer and bake for 10 minutes, until golden brown.
6. Top with blue cheese and serve.

Nutritional value per serving:

Calories: 249kcal, Fat: 14g, Carb: 18g, Proteins: 11g

Chicken and Potatoes

This crispy chicken is served over hearty air-fried purple potatoes.
Prep time and cooking time: 30 minutes| Serves: 2

Ingredients To Use:
- 1/2 cup purple sweet potato, peeled and rinsed
- 1/2 cup of salad green
- 1/2 portion of chicken, halved, rinsed, and pat dry
- 1 tsp. olive
- 1 tbsp. herbs chicken spices

Step-by-Step Directions to Cook It:
1. Combine the spices and olive oil in a large bowl. Dip in the chicken and marinate for at least 8 hours in the refrigerator.
2. Set the Air Fryer to 350°F.
3. Spray the Air Fryer basket with cooking oil and cook the potatoes in the Air Fryer for about 10 minutes.
4. Add the chicken into the Air Fryer basket and cook for about 12 minutes, until brown, nicely colored, and tender.
5. Serve with greens.

Nutritional value per serving:

Calories: 255kcal, Fat: 12g, Carb: 23g, Proteins: 16g

Chicken Nachos

Chicken nachos are arranged in a nice pile and topped with a tasty blend of Mexican shredded cheese, tomatoes, and beans.
Prep time and cooking time: 30 minutes| Serves: 4

Ingredients To Use:
- 2 medium tomatoes, seeded and diced
- 15 oz. can black beans, rinsed and drained

- 1 tsp. garlic powder
- 1 tsp. salt
- 4 scallions, chopped
- 3/4 cup chopped fresh cilantro
- 8-oz. shredded cheese, Mexican blend
- 2 tsp. chili powder
- 2 tsp. ground cumin
- 2 cups chopped or shredded cooked chicken breasts
- Tortilla chips
- 1 jalapeño, chopped

Step-by-Step Directions to Cook It:

1. Combine the chili powder, garlic powder, cumin, and salt in a small bowl.
2. Add the chicken into the mixture and toss evenly to coat.
3. Line the Air Fryer basket with aluminum foil. Arrange the chips inside the Air Fryer basket and top with the chicken, beans, tomatoes, scallion, and cheese.
4. Set the Air Fryer to 300°F and bake for 15 minutes. Garnish with cilantro and jalapeño.

Nutritional value per serving:

Calories: 295kcal, Fat: 15g, Carb: 10g, Proteins: 8g

Turkey Breast

The turkey breast is cooked to tender and then served with a mixture of sauce, sages, lemon juice, cumin pepper butter, and chives.
Prep time and cooking time: 1 hour | Serves: 4

Ingredients To Use:

- 4 tbsp. butter
- Ground pepper
- 2 tbsp. olive oil
- 1/4 tsp. ground cumin
- 1 tsp. Worcestershire sauce
- A handful of sage, chopped

- 1 lb. turkey breast steaks, pound and slice to pieces
- Kosher salt
- 1 tbsp. fresh lemon juice
- 1/4 cup chives, chopped

Step-by-Step Directions to Cook It:

1. Oil the Air Fryer basket and set the temperature of the Air Fryer to 350°F.
2. Season the turkey with pepper and salt.
3. Pulse the cumin, lemon juice, salt, sauce, chives, and salt in a blender.
4. Air fry the turkey and serve with the chives mixture.

Nutritional value per serving:

Calories: 250kcal, Fat: 10g, Carb: 5g, Proteins: 15g

Glazed Rosemary Chicken

This rich flavored glazed rosemary recipe takes your chicken to a whole new savory level.
Prep time and cooking time: 20 minutes| Serves: 2

Ingredients To Use:

- 1 spring rosemary, roughly chopped
- 1/2 tsp. red pepper flakes
- 2 tsp. honey
- 2 chicken breasts, rinsed and pat dry
- 1 tsp. olive oil
- ground pepper, to taste
- kosher salt, to taste

Step-by-Step Directions to Cook It:

1. Brush the chicken with olive oil. Season the chicken (skin-side up) with pepper, salt, red pepper, honey, and rosemary.
2. Preheat the Air Fryer to 330°F and bake the chicken for 15 minutes, until tender.

Nutritional value per serving:

Calories: 220kcal, Fat: 18g, Carb: 9g Proteins:

9g

Air Fried Butter Milk Chicken

The chicken is firstly marinated with seasoned buttermilk before air fried to crispy tenderness.

Prep time and cooking time: 8 hours 40 minutes| Serves: 4

Ingredients To Use:

- 2 chicken breasts

Marinade

- 2 cups buttermilk
- 2 tsp. salt
- 2 tsp. black pepper
- 1 tsp. cayenne pepper

Seasoned Flour

- 2 cups flour
- 1 tbsp. baking powder
- 1 tbsp. garlic powder
- 1 tbsp. paprika powder
- 1 tsp. salt
- 1 tsp. pepper

Step-by-Step Directions to Cook It:

1. To prepare the marinade, combine the pepper, salt, and chicken pieces in a large bowl. Add the buttermilk and refrigerate for at least 8 hours.
2. In another separate large bowl, mix the flour, paprika, salt, pepper, baking powder, and garlic powder. Take out the marinated chicken and discard the marinade. Coat the marinated chicken with the seasoned flour mixture.
3. Transfer the coated chicken into the Air Fryer basket and cook in a 370⁰F preheated oil-coated Air Fryer.
4. Cook the chicken for about 30 minutes and spray cooking oil at intervals.
5. Serve.

Nutritional value per serving:

Calories: 294kcal, Fat: 15g, Carb: 10g, Proteins: 18g

Sauced Chicken Wings

A simple blend of sweet-based sauces, honey, and sour wine makes funky savory glazed wings.

Prep time and cooking time: 1 hour 10 minutes| Serves: 8

Ingredients To Use:

- 1-1/2 cup of honey
- 21 pieces of chicken wings, washed and pat dry
- 1-1/2 oz. of canola oil
- 1 tsp. light soy sauce
- 3 tsp. oyster sauce
- 3 tsp. dark soy sauce
- 1/2 tsp. pepper
- Huo Tiao Chinese Wine

Step-by-Step Directions to Cook It:

1. To prepare the marinade, combine the soy sauces, Huo Tiao wine, oyster sauce, oil, pepper, and honey.
2. Transfer the marinade and chicken wings to a ziploc bag and marinate in the refrigerator for about 30 minutes. Line the Air Fryer basket with aluminum foil and arrange the chicken into it.
3. Preheat the Air Fryer to 392°F. Cook the chicken for about 30 minutes, until golden brown.

Nutritional value per serving:

Calories: 290kcal, Fat: 17g, Carb: 14g, Proteins: 19g

Chicken Jerks

This distinctive seasoned jerk recipe is made

with aromatic spices that adds a lovely flavor to the chicken.

Prep time and cooking time: 1 hour |Serves: 5

- 1 tsp. of white pepper
- 3 tsp. of chopped fresh thyme
- 6 cloves of garlic, finely diced
- 1 tsp. of cinnamon
- 4 green onions, finely chopped
- 2-1/2 ounces of lime juice
- 1 tsp. cayenne pepper
- 6 tsp. of sugar
- 30 chicken wings
- 8 tablespoons of red wine vinegar
- 6 tsp. of soy sauce
- 1 tsp. of salt
- 6 tsp. of vegetable oil
- 3 tsp. of grated ginger
- 1 habanera pepper, seeded and finely chopped

Step-by-Step Directions to Cook It:

1. Mix all the ingredients in a large glass bowl and then toss with chicken pieces. Place the bowl in the refrigerator and marinate for at least 6 hours.
2. Preheat the Air Fryer to 390ºF.
3. Take out the wings and discard the marinade.
4. Cook the chicken in the Air Fryer for about 20 minutes.
5. Drizzle ranch dressing atop chicken and serve.

Nutritional value per serving:

Calories: 220kcal, Fat: 18g, Carb: 19g, Proteins: 24g

Teriyaki Chicken Wings

If you are a lover of well-flavored chicken wings, you'll love this recipe. This teriyaki chicken wing recipe is great for parties, day out, and a big game day.

Prep time and cooking time: 50 minutes| Serves: 6

Ingredients To Use:

- 24 chicken wings, steamed
- 5 tbsp. chopped cilantro, chopped

Sauce

- 3 tbsp. rice wine vinegar
- 1/4 cup brown sugar
- 5 garlic cloves, minced
- 1 cup of soy sauce
- 1 cup of grapefruit juice
- 1/4 cup hoisin sauce
- 2 tbsp. ketchup
- 2 tbsp. fresh and grated ginger

Step-by-Step Directions to Cook It:

1. Preheat the Air Fryer to 330ºF.
2. Transfer the steamed wings into the Air Fryer and bake for about 30 minutes. Coat with cooking oil and flip at intervals.
3. Mix the sauce ingredients in a saucepan and cook over medium heat until a paste is formed.
4. Serve the chicken with sauce and sprinkle in cilantro.
5. Serve.

Nutritional value per serving:

Calories: 271.9kcal, Fat: 9.8g, Carb: 19.9g, Proteins: 24.7g

Tabasco Chicken

This tabasco chicken recipe is loaded with great flavor and made of simple ingredients easily accessible at the local grocery store.

Prep time and cooking time: 30 minutes | Serves: 4

Ingredients To Use:

- 6 chicken legs, tip trimmed off

Marinade Ingredient:

- 1 tbsp. Tabasco sauce
- 1 tbsp. ketchup
- 1 tbsp. soy sauce
- 1 tbsp. cider vinegar

Step-by-Step Directions to Cook It:

1. Combine the marinade ingredients in a small bowl and toss the chicken legs into it.
2. Preheat the Air Fryer to 330ºF.
3. Cook the chicken for about 20 minutes on both sides until golden brown.

Nutritional value per serving:

Calories: 295cal, Fat: 12g, Carb: 0.6 g, Proteins: 15g

Turkey Fritters

This easy homemade recipe is a great idea when you have a leftover turkey that needs to be used up.
Prep time and cooking time: 30 minutes|
Serves: 4

Ingredients To Use:
- 2 or 3 green chilies finely chopped
- 1-1/2 tbsp. lemon juice
- Salt and pepper to taste
- 1 lb. minced turkey
- 3 tbsp. ginger finely chopped
- 1-2 tbsp. fresh coriander leaves

Step-by-Step Directions to Cook It:

1. Combine the ingredients in a clean bowl.
2. Shape the mixture into round and flat patties using your palms.
3. Wet the patties slightly with water.
4. Set the Air Fryer to160ºF.
5. Cook the patties in the Air Fryer basket for about 30 minutes until evenly cooked.
6. Serve.

Nutritional value per serving:

Calories: 196kcal, Fat: 10g, Carb: 6g, Proteins: 15g

Duck Fingers

The recipe is another twist to the traditional chicken recipe which is loved by kids and adults.
Prep time and cooking time: 30 minutes|
Serves: 4

Ingredients To Use:
- 1 cup of milk
- 3 medium eggs
- 1 cup of rice flour
- 1 tsp. garlic powder
- Salt and pepper to taste
- 1 tsp. chili powder
- 2 duck breast, cut into strips

Step-by-Step Directions to Cook It:

1. Combine the eggs and milk in a large bowl and toss the duck strips into the bowl.
2. Mix all the remaining ingredients in another bowl and transfer the duck into the mixture.
3. Preheat the Air Fryer to 220ºF and cook the duck fingers for about 20 minutes until golden brown.
4. Serve.

Nutritional value per serving:

Calories: 195kcal, Fat: 10g, Carb: 12g, Proteins: 8g

Turkey Burger Cutlets

The turkey burger cutlet is a must-try for burger lovers. The patties can also be stored in a refrigerator overnight.
Prep time and cooking time: 30 minutes |
Serves: 4

Ingredients To Use:

- 1/2 lb. minced turkey
- 1/2 cup breadcrumbs
- A pinch of salt to taste
- 1/4 tsp. ginger finely chopped
- 1 green chili finely chopped
- 1 tsp. lemon juice
- 1 tbsp. Fresh coriander leaves, chopped
- 1/4 tsp. red chili powder
- 1/2 cup of boiled peas
- 1/4 tsp. cumin powder
- 1/4 tbsp. dried mango powder

Step-by-Step Directions to Cook It:

1. Mix all the ingredients in a large bowl. Shape the mixture into cutlets using your palms.
2. Preheat the Air Fryer to 250⁰F.
3. Cook the cutlets for about 15 minutes and stuff them in between the toasted buns.

Nutritional value per serving:

Calories: 237kcal, Fat: 15g, Carb: 10g, Proteins: 12g

Pesto Chicken

Chicken air fried with pesto is great for parties, holidays, picnics, and birthdays.
Prep time and cooking time: 40 minutes| Serves: 4

Ingredients To Use:

- 2 tbsp. olive oil
- 1/4 cup of basil pesto
- Kosher salt
- Ground cayenne pepper
- 1-1/2 lbs. chicken breast

Step-by-Step Directions to Cook It:

1. Preheat the Air Fryer to 320⁰F.
2. In a small-sized bowl, combine the pesto and oil. Set the mixture aside.
3. Oil the chicken and season it with pepper and salt.
4. Cook in the Air Fryer for about 20 minutes, until tender.
5. Serve.

Nutritional value per serving:

Calories: 180kcal, Fat:12 g, Carb: 0g, Proteins: 22g

Chicken Wrapped in Bacon

The chicken remains moist and savory wrapped in bacon and cheese before it is cooked in the Air Fryer.
Prep time and cooking time: 20 minutes | Serves: 4

Ingredients To Use:

- 1 tbsp. garlic soft cheese
- 6 Rashers unsmoked back bacon
- 1 chicken breast, chopped

Step-by-Step Directions to Cook It:

1. Spread out the bacon and lay some cheese atop it.
2. Arrange the chicken atop the bacon and cheese. Roll them up and tie up with a butcher string or a cocktail stick.
3. Place the rolled-up chicken in the Air Fryer and cook for about 15 minutes at 356⁰F.

Nutritional value per serving:

Calories: 198kcal, Fat: 7.9g, Carb: 1.5g, Proteins: 30.3g

Chicken Kiev

Be ready to savor one of the most flavourful chicken you've ever tasted with this recipe
Prep time and cooking time: 35 minutes | Serves: 2

Ingredients To Use:

- Breadcrumbs

- 1 medium chicken breast, flattened and chopped.
- 1/2 cup soft cheese
- 1/4 tsp. garlic puree
- 1tsp. parsley
- Medium egg (beaten)
- Salt and pepper, as desired

Step-by-Step Directions to Cook It:

1. Combine ½ of the parsley, garlic, and soft cheese in a small bowl.
2. Stuff the mixture in between the chicken.
3. In another small bowl, combine the salt, pepper, parsley, and bread crumbs.
4. Coat the chicken in beaten eggs and then in the bread crumbs mixture.
5. Cook the chicken in the Air Fryer at 350⁰F for about 30 minutes.
6. Serve.

Nutritional value per serving:

Calories: 322kcal, Fat: 19g, Carb: 28g, Proteins: 21g

Garlic Herb Turkey

The Air Fryer cooks this turkey recipe to a nice juicy fork-tender. For this year's Thanksgiving, don't forget to use an Air Fryer for a yummy buttery turkey.
Prep time and cooking time: 1 hour 10 minutes | Serves: 6

Ingredients To Use:
- 3 cloves garlic, minced
- 1 tsp. freshly chopped thyme
- 2 lb. turkey breast, rinsed and pat dry
- Kosher salt and pepper to taste
- 4 tbsp. butter, melted
- 1 tsp. freshly chopped rosemary

Step-by-Step Directions to Cook It:
1. Season the turkey with pepper and salt.
2. Mix the thyme, rosemary and butter in a small bowl.
3. Transfer the turkey to oil-coated Air Fryer basket and cook at 380⁰F for about 40 minutes.
4. Flip the turkey at intervals and cook until fork-tender.
5. Rest on a platter before serving.

Nutritional value per serving:

Calories: 226kcal, Fat: 19g, Carb: 5g, Proteins: 34g

Chicken Breast with Tarragon Mustard Paste

This recipe is a no-brainer weekend dinner delight. You can boost its flavor by marinating the chicken breasts.
Prep time and cooking time: 20minutes| Serves: 4

Ingredients To Use:
- 1 cup Dijon mustard
- 2 tbsp. olive oil
- 1/2 tsp. ground pepper
- 4 chicken breast, halved, boned, and skinned
- 1 tbsp. dried tarragon leaves

Step-by-Step Directions to Cook It:
1. Combine all the ingredients and then set aside.
2. Preheat the Air Fryer to 320⁰F.
3. Transfer the chicken to the Air Fryer and cook for about 10 minutes, and flip the chicken to the other side at intervals.
4. Serve.

Nutritional value per serving:

Calories: 202kcal, Fat: 8g, Carb: 4g, Proteins: 18g

Hoisin Glazed Chicken Thighs

The sauce gives the chicken thighs a sweet,

smoky flavor. The recipe is best served with rice.

Prep time and cooking time: 20 minutes|
Serves: 4

Ingredients To Use:

- 8 chicken thighs
- Olive oil
- Sea salt
- Ground black pepper
- 1-1/2 hoisin ginger sauce

Step-by-Step Directions to Cook It:

1. Rinse the chicken thighs and pat dry with a paper towel. Season them with pepper and salt. Coat the chicken with oil and transfer to a preheated Air Fryer.
2. Brush the sauce atop chicken and cook for about 15 minutes at 320⁰F.
3. Brush the sauce atop chicken frequently at intervals until fork-tender.
4. Serve.

Nutritional value per serving:

Calories: 242kcal, Fat: 15g, Carb: 5g, Proteins: 19g

BlackBerry Glazed Chicken

This fruit-infused chicken recipe is rich in antioxidants, giving you a healthy and tasty experience.

Prep time and cooking time: 30 minutes|
Serves: 4

Ingredients To Use:

- 6 oz. fresh blackberries
- 1/4 cup of water
- 2 tbsp. white wine vinegar
- 1 tbsp. sugar
- 2 tbsp. cold butter
- 1 tbsp. whole-grain mustard
- 4 chicken thighs, rinsed and pat dried
- 4 drumsticks, rinsed and pat dried

- Sea salt and ground black pepper to taste
- Fresh, flat-leaf parsley

Step-by-Step Directions to Cook It:

1. Preheat the Air Fryer to 340⁰F.
2. Spray the Air Fryer basket with cooking oil.
3. In a small-medium skill, add berries, water, sugar, and vinegar. Cook for about 10 minutes and mash the berries with a potato masher. Continue cooking until half of the liquid is vapored. Add the mustard and cold butter. Set aside.
4. Dip the chicken into the berry mixture and cook in the Air Fryer to fork-tender. Baste the chicken occasionally while cooking.
5. Enjoy!

Nutritional value per serving:

Calories: 182kcal, Fat: 8g, Carb: 4g, Proteins: 12g

Popcorn Chicken

Cut into a bite-size, the air fired chicken is always welcomed by kids. Enjoy with the dipping sauce!

Prep time and cooking time: 10 minutes |
Serves: 4

Ingredients To Use:

- 1-1/2 lbs. chicken thighs, boneless and skinless
- 1 egg
- 1 cup of flour
- 1 tsp. baking powder
- 1 cup canola oil
- 1 cup of pickle brine
- Salt to taste

Step-by-Step Directions to Cook It:

1. Marinate the chicken in pickle juice and refrigerate for some hours.
2. Whisk the egg and milk in a bowl.
3. Combine the flour, salt and baking powder in a large bowl.
4. Coat the chicken in the egg and milk before dipping in the flour mixture.
5. Shake the chicken to remove the excessive flour.
6. Fry the chicken in the Air Fryer for 3 minutes at 350⁰F.
7. Serve.

Nutritional value per serving:

Calories: 327kcal, Fat: 22g, Carb: 10g, Proteins: 25g

Keto Fried Chicken

Are you looking for a recipe that allows you to enjoy fried chicken? Then you have to try out this recipe.
Prep time and cooking time: 4 hours 10 minutes | Serves: 4

Ingredients To Use:
- 1-1/2 lb. chicken drumsticks
- 1 tsp. paprika
- 2 eggs
- Canola oil
- 1/4 tsp. cayenne pepper
- 1 cup almond flour
- Salt to taste
- 3/4 cup of whipping cream

Step-by-Step Directions to Cook It:
1. Combine the chicken and whipping cream in a bowl. Refrigerate for about 4 hours.
2. Preheat the Air Fryer to 35o⁰F.
3. Mix the almond flour, salt, and pepper in a bowl.
4. Dip the chicken in the egg mixture and then flour mixture.
5. Air fry the chicken for 10 minutes until golden brown.

Nutritional value per serving:

Calories: 312kcal, Fat: 18g, Carb: 1g, Proteins: 25g

Chicken and Sweet Potatoes

The combo of creamy flavored chicken and potatoes is everything you want in a comforting meal.
Prep time and cooking time: 40 minutes | Serves: 4

Ingredients To Use:
- 5 oz. chicken breast
- 3 tsp. of vegetable oil
- Salt and pepper to taste
- 1/4 cup of flour, seasoned with salt and pepper
- 1 cup of buttermilk
- 1 tsp. of garlic, finely chopped
- 1 egg, whisked
- 1/2 tsp. of pepper
- 7 oz. of breadcrumbs
- 2 medium-sized sweet potatoes, peel, and slice into chips.
- 3 tsp. of smoked paprika

Step-by-Step Directions to Cook It:
1. Combine the garlic, buttermilk, and pepper into the bowl of chicken breasts.
2. Marinate the chicken in the fridge for at least 6 hours.
3. Set the Air Fryer to 374⁰F.
4. Remove the marinated chicken and discard the marinade.
5. Coat the chicken in flour, egg, and seasoned bread crumbs.
6. Transfer the chicken into the Air Fryer and cook for about 10 minutes. Set aside.
7. Cook the potatoes in an Air Fryer for

about 6 minutes and then season with salt and pepper.

8. Serve the chicken with chips.

Nutritional value per serving:

Calories: 298kcal, Fat: 12g, Carb: 18g, Proteins: 16g

Chicken with Buttered Pecan

Pecan adds floral and woodsy aroma to the recipe. It's also loaded with iron, fiber, and calcium.

Prep time and cooking time: 45 minutes| Serves: 4

Ingredients To Use:

- 2 tbsp. packed brown sugar
- Zest of 1 lemon
- 1/2 tsp. ground cayenne (optional)
- 1 tsp. freshly ground black pepper
- Cooking spray
- 3 1/2 cups of pecans, finely chopped
- 4 tbsp. butter, melted, divided
- 2 large eggs
- 1 1/4 lb. chicken breast, chopped
- 1/4 cup of all-purpose flour
- 1/2 tsp. kosher salt

Step-by-Step Directions to Cook It:

1. Preheat the Air Fryer to 425°F. Spray the Air Fryer basket with cooking oil.
2. Put the chopped pecans in a bowl and set aside.
3. In another bowl, combine the sugar, lemon zest, pepper, melted butter, and egg.
4. Dip the chicken in the flour mixture and dredge in the egg mixture.
5. Roll the pecans on the chicken and transfer the chicken to the Air Fryer basket.
6. Cook for about 15 minutes and brush butter on the chicken at intervals.

7. Season with salt. Garnish with parsley and drizzle honey mustard atop it.

Nutritional value per serving:

Calories: 222kcal, Fat: 15g, Carb: 8g, Proteins: 18g

Chicken Salad

Fresh herbs give this recipe a fun twist. You can either poach the chicken or air fry it to your taste.

Prep time and cooking time: 30 minutes | Serves: 4

Ingredients To Use:

- 1/2 cup of mayonnaise
- 1/2 cup small dill pickle, chopped
- 2 tbsp. pickle brine
- Kosher salt and freshly ground black pepper
- 2 stalks celery, sliced
- 2 tbsp. chopped fresh flat-leaf parsley
- 2 tbsp. chopped fresh dill
- 1-1/2 lb. boneless, skinless chicken breast

Step-by-Step Directions to Cook It:

1. Preheat the Air Fryer to 340°F.
2. Coat the Air Fryer basket with cooking oil.
3. Season the chicken breast with pepper and salt.
4. Cook the chicken in the Air Fryer till fork-tender and then shred into pieces. Set aside and allow to cool.
5. Combine all the remaining ingredients in a small bowl.
6. Add the shredded chicken and serve.

Nutritional value per serving:

Calories: 196kcal, Fat: 13g, Carb: 6g, Proteins: 12g

Air Fried Chicken with Tomatoes and Fennel Seed

The air fried chicken is cooked with lots of flavourful and colorful veggies that are hard to resist.

Prep time and cooking time: 1 hour 10 minutes | Serves: 4

Ingredients To Use:

- 1 tbsp. lemon zest
- 3 tbsp. lemon juice
- 4 lbs. chicken, flattened and bone removed
- 3 tbsp. lemon juice
- 1 cup grape tomatoes, rinsed
- 1 cup pitted olives
- 8 oz. sourdough bread, shredded into 1-inch pieces
- 3 cup baby kale
- 2 fennel bulbs, cored and sliced
- 1 garlic clove, crushed
- 3 tbsp. olive oil
- Kosher salt and freshly ground pepper to taste
- 1 tbsp. fennel seeds, crushed
- 1 tbsp. coriander seeds, crushed

Step-by-Step Directions to Cook It:

1. Preheat the Air Fryer to 450°F. Line the Air Fryer tray with aluminum foil. Combine the garlic, fennel, garlic, and one spoonful of oil inside the Air Fryer tray. Sprinkle in salt and pepper.
2. Brush the chicken with oil and then add the spice mixture.
3. Lower the Air Fryer temperature to 360⁰F. Place tomatoes and olives into the Air Fryer tray and arrange the chicken atop them. Cook for about 30 minutes.
4. Mix the bread and the remaining oil in a bowl. Add salt and pepper. Sprinkle the bread mixture into air fried chicken and continue cooking till fork-tender.
5. Place the chicken on a platter and serve with kale. Drizzle some lemon juice if desired.

Nutritional value per serving:

Calories: 216kcal, Fat: 14g, Carb: 6g, Proteins: 18g

Curry Chicken Salad

The recipe gets its bright color from the traditional curry spice. Pack this homemade meal for a nice sunny picnic day.

Prep time and cooking time: 30 minutes | Serves: 4

Ingredients To Use:

- 2 scallions, thinly sliced
- 1/4 cup of fresh cilantro, chopped
- 1/4 cup low-fat sour cream
- 2 tbsp. mayonnaise
- 1 tsp. lemon zest
- 2 tbsp. fresh lemon juice
- 1 tbsp. curry powder
- Kosher salt and freshly ground black pepper
- 1/2 cup of golden raisins
- 1-1/2 lb. boneless, skinless chicken breast, chopped

Step-by-Step Directions to Cook It:

1. Preheat the Air Fryer to 340⁰F.
2. Coat the Air Fryer basket with cooking oil.
3. Season the chicken breast with pepper and salt.
4. Cook the chicken in the Air Fryer till fork-tender and then shred into pieces. Set aside and allow to cool.
5. Combine all the remaining ingredients in a small bowl.
6. Add the shredded chicken and serve.

Calories: 112kcal, Fat: 14g, Carb: 4g, Proteins: 12g

Air Fried Cornflakes Crusted Chicken

Cornflakes add a fun crunchy texture to chicken recipes. The air fried chicken is extra crispy and also requires no extra oil.

Prep time and cooking time: 1 hour 30 minutes | Serves: 4

Ingredients To Use:

- 4 small bone-in chicken thighs, skin removed
- 1 cup all-purpose flour
- 1/2 tsp. cayenne pepper
- Sea salt and ground black pepper to taste
- 4 small chicken drumsticks, skin removed
- 4 cup crunchy cornflakes cereal, crushed
- 1 tsp. celery seed, divided

Step-by-Step Directions to Cook It:

1. Preheat the Air Fryer to 360°F. Add the garlic powder, celery seed, buttermilk, salt, and cayenne seed in a glass bowl. Toss the mixture with chicken and marinate for 30 minutes in a refrigerator.
2. Line the Air Fryer tray with aluminum foil and coat with oil.
3. Mix pepper, salt flour, and the remaining celery seed in a bowl and set aside.
4. Pour the remaining buttermilk in another bowl and do the same for cornflakes.
5. Take out the chicken from the marinade and coat firstly in flour, buttermilk, and then crushed cornflakes.
6. Arrange the coated chicken in the Air Fryer basket and cook for about 30 minutes until fork-tender.
7. Serve.

Nutritional value per serving:

Calories: 222kcal, Fat: 8g, Carb: 15g, Proteins: 16g

Jerk Chicken and Mango Lettuce Ball

The recipe is sweet, low carb, and has quite a nice blend of texture. Get your jerk chicken to a whole new level!

Prep time and cooking time: 40 minutes| Serves: 4

Ingredients To Use:

- 1-1/2 tbsp. soy sauce
- 2 tsp. jerk seasoning
- 2 chopped garlic cloves
- 1 tsp. jarred fresh ginger
- 3/4 cup chopped mango
- 1/4 cup chopped fresh cilantro leaves
- 1 cup of basmati rice, cooked
- 1 cup chicken stock
- Kosher salt and black pepper to taste
- 1 lb. ground chicken
- 1/2 red onion, chopped
- 1/2 red bell pepper, chopped
- 1 tbsp. canola oil
- Butter lettuce leaves, for serving

Step-by-Step Directions to Cook It:

1. Line the Air Fryer basket with aluminium foil.
2. Combine the ground chicken, red bell pepper, and onion in a bowl. Season with salt and spray cooking oil atop it. Cook in the Air Fryer for about 20 minutes at 250⁰F, until golden brown.
3. Meanwhile, heat the canola oil in a large skillet. Add the soy sauce, clove, jerk

seasoning, and ginger. Cook until fragrant and season with pepper.

4. Fold the sauce mixture into mango and cilantro. Stuff the chicken and rice in buttercup leaves. Serve.

Calories: 195kcal, Fat: 12g, Carb: 6g, Proteins: 19g

Kale and Chicken Pita Salad

The pita just adds a great layer of crunchiness to the Mediterranean kale chicken salad recipe.
Prep time and cooking time: 30 minutes|
Serves: 4

Ingredients To Use:
- 1 chopped garlic clove
- 5-oz. container baby kale
- 2 cup lightly crushed pita chips
- 2 sliced scallions
- 1-1/2 lb. chicken tenders
- 2 tsp. salt-free Greek seasoning
- Kosher salt and black pepper
- 3-1/2 tbsp. olive oil
- 3 tbsp. fresh lemon juice
- 2 tbsp. tahini
- 2 sliced Persian cucumbers
- 5 thinly sliced radishes
- 1 cup halved grape tomatoes

Step-by-Step Directions to Cook It:
1. Preheat the Air Fryer to 340⁰F.
2. Coat the Air Fryer basket with cooking oil.
3. Season the chicken breast with pepper and salt.
4. Cook the chicken in the Air Fryer till

fork-tender and then shred into pieces. Set aside and allow to cool.

5. Combine all the remaining ingredients in a small bowl.
6. Add the shredded chicken and serve.

Nutritional value per serving:

Calories: 175kcal, Fat: 8g, Carb: 12g, Proteins: 22g

Cheese Stuffed Chicken

Cheesy chicken is a fantastic dish that'll wow your guest right away. The recipe is a sure take-home-to-mama.
Prep time and cooking time: 35 minutes|
Serves: 4

Ingredients To Use:
- 1 cup quartered cherry tomatoes
- 2 oz. crumbled goat cheese
- 2 tbsp. toasted pine nuts
- 2 tbsp. chopped fresh basil
- 8 oz. boneless, skinless chicken breasts, cut "2-x-4" pocket into the chicken breast

Step-by-Step Directions to Cook It:
1. Combine the remaining ingredients in a mixing bowl and stuff inside the chicken.
2. Sprinkle in salt and pepper. Brush oil atop the chicken and set aside.
3. Preheat the Air Fryer to 360⁰F.
4. Place the chicken in the Air Fryer basket and cook until golden brown.
5. Serve.

Nutritional value per serving:

Calories: 185kcal, Fat: 12g, Carb: 6g, Proteins: 12g

Chapter 3: Fish and Seafood Recipes

Spanish Salmon

Spanish salmon is a dish that is full of vibrant flavors that you will never fail to enjoy. It is tasty and yummy!
Prep time and cooking time: 25 minutes|
Serves: 6

Ingredients To Use:

- 6 salmon fillets
- 3 red onions (cut into medium wedges)
- 2 tbsp. chopped parsley
- 1/2 tsp. smoked paprika
- 3/4 cup pitted green olives
- 5 tbsp. olive oil
- 3 red pepper cut into medium wedges
- 2 cups bread croutons
- Salt and black pepper to taste

Step-by-Step Directions to Cook It:

1. Preheat the air fryer to 356^{0}F.
2. In a pan that fits into the air fryer, add croutons, paprika, bell pepper, olives, and olive oil. Stir well and transfer to the air fryer, cook for 7 minutes.
3. Meanwhile, sprinkle the salmon with oil, and transfer to the air fryer with the veggies. Turn up the temperature to 360^{0}F. Set the time for 8 minutes.
4. Serve the fish with the veggies.

Nutritional value per serving:

Calories: 311kcal, Fat: 8g, Carb: 21g, Proteins: 22g

Delicious Red Snapper

The herbs and vegetables complement the nutty flavor of the red snapper, creating a mouth-watering dish.
Prep time and cooking time: 45 minutes|
Serves: 4

Ingredients To Use:

- 1 big red snapper
- 1 jalapeno (chopped)
- 3 cloves garlic (minced)
- 1 red bell pepper (chopped)
- 1 tbsp. butter
- 2 tbsp. white wine
- 2 tbsp. chopped parsley
- 1/2 lb. chopped okra
- Salt and pepper to taste

Step-by-Step Directions to Cook It:

1. In a bowl, mix the jalapeno, wine, and stir. Rub the snapper with the mixture and season with salt and pepper. Leave to marinate for 30 minutes.
2. Preheat the air fryer to 400^{0}F.
3. Heat the butter in a pan over medium heat, add okra, and bell pepper. Stir and cook for 5 minutes. Stuff the red snapper with the okra mixture and parsley. Rub with olive oil and transfer to the air fryer basket, close the lid, and set the time for 15 minutes.
4. Serve and Enjoy!

Nutritional value per serving:

Calories: 261kcal, Fat: 7g, Carb: 21g, Proteins: 18g

Shrimp and Crab Mix

What can be better than the combination of crabs and shrimps? This recipe creates a meal packed full of delicious taste and nutrients.

Prep time and cooking time: 35 minutes|
Serves: 4

Ingredients To Use:

- 1 lb. shrimps (peeled and deveined)
- 1 cup chopped green bell pepper
- 1 cup flaked crabmeat
- 1 cup chopped celery
- 2 tbsp. breadcrumbs
- 1 cup mayonnaise
- 1/2 cup yellow onions (chopped)
- 1 tbsp. melted butter
- 1 tsp. Worcestershire sauce
- 1 tsp. sweet paprika
- 1 cup chopped celery
- Salt and black pepper

Step-by-Step Directions to Cook It:

1. Preheat the air fryer to 320^0F.
2. In a pan that fits into the air fryer, mix all the ingredients. Transfer to the air fryer and set the time for 25 minutes.
3. Serve and enjoy!

Nutritional value per serving:

Calories: 200kcal, Fat: 11g, Carb: 1519g, Proteins: g

Creamy Shrimps and Veggies

This dish takes shrimp dishes to a whole new level with its attractive look and flavorful tastes.
Prep time and cooking time: 40 minutes|
Serves: 4

Ingredients To Use:

- 1 lb. shrimp (peeled and deveined)
- 1 cup heavy cream
- 1 spaghetti squash (halved)
- 1 bunch of asparagus (chopped)
- 1 cup grated parmesan cheese
- 2 tbsp. olive oil

- 1/4 cup melted butter
- 2 garlic cloves (minced)
- 1 yellow onion (chopped)
- 2 tsp. Italian seasoning
- 1 tsp. red pepper flakes (crushed)
- 8 oz. mushroom (chopped)
- Salt and pepper to taste

Step-by-Step Directions to Cook It:

1. Preheat the air fryer to 390^0F, place the squash halves in the air fryer basket. Close the lid and cook for 17 minutes. Transfer to a board and scoop the inside into a bowl.
2. Boil enough water in a pot over medium heat, add asparagus for 2-3 minutes. Transfer to a bowl containing ice water and set aside. Heat oil in a pan that fits into the air fryer; add onions, mushroom, and cook for 7 minutes.
3. Add the remaining ingredients, and transfer to the air fryer, reduce to 360^0F. Set time to 6 minutes.
4. Serve and enjoy!

Nutritional value per serving:

Calories: 311kcal, Fat: 6g, Carb: 12g, Proteins: 16g

Salmon and Avocado Salsa

Salmon and avocado salsa is one of the best vegetable recipes available. It is healthy and full of flavors.
Prep time and cooking time: 40 minutes|
Serves: 4

Ingredients To Use:

- 4 salmon fillets
- 1 tsp. garlic powder
- 1 tbsp. olive oil
- 1/2 tsp. sweet paprika
- 1 tsp. ground cumin
- 1/2 tsp. chili powder

- Salt and pepper to taste

For the Salsa:
- 2 tbsp. chopped cilantro
- 1 red onion (chopped)
- Juice from 2 limes
- 1 avocado (peeled and chopped)
- Salt and black pepper to taste

Step-by-Step Directions to Cook It:
1. Preheat the air fryer to 350^{0}F.
2. In a medium bowl, add the onion powder, pepper, salt, chili powder, cumin, and paprika. Mix well and rub the salmon with the mixture, drizzle with oil. Transfer to the air fryer and cook for 5 minutes.
3. Meanwhile, in a bowl, add all the salsa ingredients and toss well.
4. Serve and enjoy.

Nutritional value per serving:

Calories: kcal, Fat: g, Carb: g, Proteins: g

Salmon and Greek Yogurt Sauce

The salmon and Greek yogurt sauce are creamy, tasty, and delicious. It can be easily prepared.
Prep time and cooking time: 30 minutes|
Serves: 2

Ingredients To Use:
- 2 salmon fillets
- 1 cup Greek yogurt
- 1 tbsp. chopped basil
- 1/2 tsp. chopped cilantro
- 6 lemon slices
- 1/2 tsp. chopped mint
- 2 tsp. curry powder
- 1 garlic clove (pressed)
- Pinch of cayenne pepper
- Salt and pepper to taste

Step-by-Step Directions to Cook It:

1. Preheat the air fryer to 400^{0}F.
2. Place each salmon fillet on parchment paper, make 3 slits, and stuff with basil. Season the fillets with salt and pepper, top each with a slice of lemon. Fold parchment paper and seal, transfer to the air fryer and bake for 20 minutes.
3. Meanwhile, in a bowl, add the yogurt, pepper, cayenne pepper, curry, garlic, mint, cilantro, and salt. Mix well.
4. Serve the fish drizzled with the yogurt sauce.

Nutritional value per serving:

Calories: 242kcal, Fat: 1g, Carb: 2g, Proteins: 8g

Asian Halibut

The Asian halibut is mouth-watering and delicious. It is best served with steamed rice.
Prep time and cooking time: 40 minutes|
Serves: 3

Ingredients To Use:
- 1 lb. halibut Steaks
- 1/4 cup sugar
- 1/2 cup mirin
- 2/3 cup soy sauce
- 2 tbsp. lime juice
- 1/4 cup orange juice
- 1 garlic clove (minced)
- 1/4 tsp. red pepper flakes (crushed)
- 1 tsp. grated ginger

Step-by-Step Directions to Cook It:

1. Place a pot over medium heat and add the soy sauce and other ingredients except for the fish. Bring to a boil and remove from heat. Pour half of the marinade into a bowl, add the halibut, and stir. Leave to marinate in the refrigerator for 30 minutes.

2. Preheat the air fryer to 390^0F.
3. Transfer to the air fryer and cook for 10 minutes, flip in between the cooking. Serve the halibut with the rest of the sauce.
4. Enjoy!

Nutritional value per serving:

Calories: 251kcal, Fat: 5g, Carb: 14g, Proteins: 23g

Flavour Air Fried Salmon

Salmon is an everyday favorite with its subtle flavor and great taste. Cooking this with an air fryer for a healthy meal.
Prep time and cooking time: 1 hour 8 minutes| Serves: 2

Ingredients To Use:

- 2 salmon fillets
- 1/3 cup brown sugar
- 2 tbsp. lemon juice
- 1/3 cup water
- 1/2 tsp. garlic powder
- 1/3 cup brown sugar
- 3 scallions, chopped
- 2 tbsp. olive oil
- Salt and black pepper to taste

Step-by-Step Directions to Cook It:

1. In a bowl, add the sugar, water, garlic, lemon juice, soy sauce, salt, pepper, and oil. Whisk until well combined; add the salmon fillets and mix. Leave to marinate for 1 hour.
2. Transfer the salmon fillets to your air fryer and cook for 8 minutes, flip in between the cooking.
3. Serve garnished with scallions, enjoy!

Nutritional value per serving:

Calories: 160kcal, Fat: 8g, Carb: 20g, Proteins: 21g

Salmon with Capers and Mashed Potatoes

The salmon with capers and mashed potatoes is a quick and easy meal to satisfy your guests.
Prep time and cooking time: 30 minutes| Serves: 4

Ingredients To Use:

- 4 salmon fillets (skinless and boneless)
- 2 tsp. olive oil
- 1 tbsp. capers (drained)
- Juice from 1 lemon
- Salt and black pepper to taste

For the Potato Mash:

- 1/2 cup milk
- 2 tbsp. olive oil
- 1 lb. potatoes (peeled and chopped)
- 1 tbsp. dried dill

Step-by-Step Directions to Cook It:

1. Preheat the air fryer to 360^0F.
2. Put potatoes in a pot, add water and salt, bring to a boil over medium heat for 15 minutes. Drain and transfer to a bowl and mash using a potato masher. Add 2 tbsp. oil, milk, dill, salt, and pepper. Whisk well and set aside.
3. Season the salmon with salt, pepper, and oil. Transfer to your air fryer basket, top with capers and cook for 8 minutes.
4. Serve and enjoy!

Nutritional value per serving:

Calories: 270kcal, Fat: 16g, Carb: 8g, Proteins: 16g

Lemony Saba Fish

This recipe creates a crusty and flaky fish; you are going to enjoy the subtle taste of this fish lingering on your palate.

Prep time and cooking time: 18 minutes|
Serves: 1

Ingredients To Use:

- 4 Saba fish fillets (boneless)
- 2 tbsp. lemon juice
- 2 tbsp. olive oil
- 3 red chili pepper, (chopped)
- 2 tbsp. garlic (minced)
- Salt and black pepper to taste

Step-by-Step Directions to Cook It:

1. Preheat the air fryer to 360^0F.
2. Season the fish with salt, pepper, lemon juice, chili, garlic, and oil. Toss to coat, transfer to the air fryer and cook for 8 minutes, flipping halfway.
3. Serve and Enjoy!

Nutritional value per serving:

Calories: 290kcal, Fat: 4g, Carb: 6g, Proteins: 15g

Honey Sea Bass

The sea bass is a tasty and flavourful fish dish that is easy to prepare. The herbs and spices blended with the fish create a great flavor.
Prep time and cooking time: 20 minutes|
Serves: 2

Ingredients To Use:

- 2 sea bass fillets
- 2 tbsp. mustard
- Zest from 1/2 orange, grated
- 1/2 lb. canned lentils, drained
- Juice from 1/2 orange
- 2 tbsp. olive oil
- 2 oz. watercress
- 2 tsp. honey
- A small bunch of parsley (chopped)
- A small bunch of dill (chopped)
- Salt and black pepper to taste

Step-by-Step Directions to Cook It:

1. Preheat the air fryer to 350^0F.
2. In a bowl, add the orange zest, 1 tbsp of oil, juice, mustard, honey, and mix. Season the fillets with salt pepper. Rub the whole fillets with the honey mixture and transfer to the air fryer cooking basket. Close the lid and set the time for 10 minutes.
3. Meanwhile, place a pot over medium heat, add the lentils and boil for 1 minute. Add the rest of the oil, parsley, dill, watercress, and stir.
4. Serve with the fish and Enjoy!

Nutritional value per serving:

Calories: 160kcal, Fat: 3g, Carb: 2g, Proteins: 16g

Delicious French Cod

The combination of various herbs creates a creamy and tasty dish that's unforgettable.
Prep time and cooking time: 32 minutes|
Serves: 4

Ingredients To Use:

- 2 lb. cod (boneless)
- 2 garlic cloves (minced)
- 2 tbsp. butter
- 3 tbsp. chopped Parsley
- 2 tbsp. olive oil
- 1/2 cup white wine
- 14 oz. canned tomatoes (stewed)
- Salt and black pepper to taste
- 1 yellow onion (chopped)

Step-by-Step Directions to Cook It:

1. Preheat the air fryer to 350^0F.
2. Heat oil in a pan over medium heat, add onions and garlic and stir until it is fragrant and translucent. Add the wine and cook for another 1 minute; add the tomatoes and cook for another 2

minutes. Remove from heat and stir in the parsley.

3. Pour the mixture into a pan that fits into the air fryer, add the fish, and season with salt and pepper. Transfer to the air fryer ad closes the lid. Set the time for 14 minutes.
4. Serve the fish with the tomato sauce, enjoy!

Nutritional value per serving:

Calories: 215kcal, Fat: 5g, Carb: 16g, Proteins: 26g

Coconut Tilapia

This recipe is simple and easy to make; it is also creamy and infused with coconut flavor.
Prep time and cooking time: 20 minutes|
Serves: 4

Ingredients To Use:
- 4 medium tilapia fillets
- 1/2 jalapeno, chopped
- 1/2 cup of chopped cilantro
- 1/2 tsp. garam masala
- 2 garlic cloves, chopped
- 1 tsp. grated ginger
- 1/2 cup of coconut milk
- Salt and black pepper to taste
- Cooking spray

Step-by-Step Directions to Cook It:
1. Preheat the air fryer to 4000^0F.
2. In a food processor, add the coconut milk and other ingredients except for the fillets and pulse well. Spray the fish with cooking spray; add the fillets to the coconut mixture. Make sure that they are well coated, transfer to the air fryer cooking basket, and close the lid. Set the time for 10 minutes.
3. Serve hot and enjoy!

Nutritional value per serving:

Calories: 200kcal, Fat: 3g, Carb: 18g, Proteins: 26g

Special Catfish Fillets

This delicious delight is crispy on the outside, flaky on the inside. It can be enjoyed as a light lunch.
Prep time and cooking time: 22 minutes|
Serves: 4

Ingredients To Use:
- 2 catfish fillets
- 2 oz. butter
- 4 oz. Worcestershire sauce
- 3/4 cup ketchup
- 1 tsp. mustard
- 1/2 tsp. jerk seasoning
- 1 tbsp. Balsamic vinegar
- 1/2 tsp. minced garlic
- 1 tbsp. chopped parsley
- Salt and black pepper to taste

Step-by-Step Directions to Cook It:
1. Preheat the air fryer to 350^0F.
2. In a pan over medium heat, heat the butter and stir in Worcestershire sauce, vinegar, seasoning, ketchup, mustard, garlic, salt, and pepper. Remove from heat and add the fish fillets. Toss well and leave to marinate for 10 minutes, drain the fish.
3. Transfer them to the air fryer, set the time for 8minutes. Flip the fillets halfway through.
4. Serve garnished with parsley.

Nutritional value per serving:

Calories: 251kcal, Fat: 3g, Carb: 20g, Proteins: 21g

Oriental Fish

The oriental fish is a combination of different spices in one dish. Air frying the fish creates a unique but attractive flavor.

Prep time and cooking time: 22 minutes|
Serves: 4

Ingredients To Use:

- 2 lb. red snapper fillets (boneless)
- 1 tbsp. lemon juice
- 1 yellow onion
- 1 tbsp. oriental sesame oil
- 2 tbsp. water
- 1 tbsp. tamarind paste
- 1/2 tsp. ground cumin
- 3 tbsp. chopped mint leaves
- 1 tbsp. grated ginger
- 3 cloves garlic (minced)
- Salt and pepper to taste

Step-by-Step Directions to Cook It:

1. Preheat the air fryer to 320^0F.
2. In a food processor, add all the ingredients except the fish and lemon juice. Pulse until a smooth consistency is achieved. Coat the fish with the mixture.
3. Transfer the fish into the air fryer and close the lid. Cook the fish for 12 minutes, flip halfway through.
4. Drizzle with the lemon juice and serve.

Nutritional value per serving:

Calories: 241kcal, Fat: 8g, Carb: 15g, Proteins: 12g

Tasty Pollock

This is a nice recipe to prepare when you are bored with your regular meals. Your palate will feel comforted with this dish.

Prep time and cooking time: 25 minutes|
Serves: 6

Ingredients To Use:

- 4 pollocks fillets (boneless)
- 2 tbsp. butter

- 1/2 cup sour cream
- 1/2 cup grated parmesan
- Salt and pepper to taste
- Cooking spray

Step-by-Step Directions to Cook It:

1. Preheat the air fryer to 320^0F.
2. In a bowl, mix all the ingredients except the pollock fillet and cooking spray. Spray the fillets with cooking spray and season with salt and pepper. Spread the sour cream mixture on the fillet and arrange in the air fryer. Close the lid and set the time for 15 minutes.
3. Serve and enjoy with salad.

Nutritional value per serving:

Calories: 290kcal, Fat: 13g, Carb: 12g, Proteins: 42g

Baked Shrimp Scampi

Baked shrimp scampi is a fancy dish that can be prepared for special occasions. The shrimps are tender and cooked to perfection.
Prep time and cooking time: 20 minutes|
Serves: 4

Ingredients To Use:

- 1 lb. large shrimps
- 3/4 cup breadcrumbs
- 1/4 cup white wine
- 8 tbsp. butter (melted)
- 1/4 tsp. paprika
- 1/2 tsp. onion powder
- 1/4 tsp. cayenne pepper
- 1 tbsp. minced garlic
- 1/2 tsp. salt

Step-by-Step Directions to Cook It:

1. Preheat the Air fryer to 350^0F.
2. In a bowl, mix breadcrumbs, onion powder, paprika, cayenne pepper, salt, and set aside. In another bowl, mix the

melted butter, garlic, and white wine. Stir in the shrimps and breadcrumbs mixture. Transfer to a casserole dish that fits into the air fryer.

3. Close the air fryer lid and set the time for 10 minutes.
4. Open the lid and serve. Enjoy!

Coconut Shrimp with Dip

This is a recipe you can easily get addicted to, which is crispy on the outside, juicy on the inside.
Prep time and cooking time: 20 minutes| Serves: 4

Ingredients To Use:

- 1 lb. raw shrimps (peeled and deveined)
- Oil for spraying
- 2 eggs beaten
- 1 tsp. salt
- 1/2 cup all-purpose flout
- 1/2 cup shredded coconut (unsweetened)
- 1/4 tsp. black pepper
- 1/4 cup panko breadcrumbs

Step-by-Step Directions to Cook It:

1. Preheat the air fryer to 390^0F.
2. In a bowl, mix the coconut, breadcrumbs, black pepper, and salt, set aside. In another two bowls, add the flour to one bowl and beaten eggs to the other.
3. Dip the shrimps in the flour, followed by the eggs and finally the coconut mixture (ensure the shrimps are well coated with all the mixture).
4. Place the shrimp on a greased tray and transfer into the air fryer, spray with oil, and cover with the lid. Set the time for 4

minutes. Open the air fryer and flip the shrimps, respray with oil and cook for another 5 minutes.

5. Serve and enjoy with Thai sweet chili sauce.

Air Fryer White Fish

Crispy and crusty, this tasty air-fried fish is as tasty as it looks. From the ingredients to the preparation, it all creates a wonderful dish.
Prep time and cooking time: 30 minutes| Serves: 4

Ingredients To Use:

- 4 white fish fillets (halved)
- 1 tsp. paprika
- 2 tbsp. olive oil
- Fish seasoning
- 1/2 tsp. black pepper
- 3/4 cup fine cornmeal
- 1/2 tsp. garlic powder
- 1/4 cup flour
- 1/2 tsp. black pepper
- 2 tsp. old bay

Step-by-Step Directions to Cook It:

1. Preheat the air fryer to 400^0F.
2. Add all the ingredients except the olive oil to a ziploc bag and set aside. Rinse the fish and pat dry with a paper towel. Place the fish fillets in the ziploc bag and shake to coat or until totally covered with the seasoning.
3. Grease the air fryer basket tray and arrange the fish on it. Close the air fryer lid and set the time for 10 minutes. Open the air fryer lid and spray both sides of the fish with oil. Cook for an additional 7 minutes, flip halfway through.

4. Serve and enjoy!

Nutritional value per serving:

Calories: 193kcal, Fat: 1g, Carb: 21g, Proteins: 20g

Lobster Tail

The recipe is lovely for the holidays, and it is also quite easy to prepare.
Prep time and cooking time: 15 minutes|
Serves: 2

Ingredients To Use:

- 2 (6 oz.) lobster tail
- 1 tsp. lemon juice
- 2 tbsp. unsalted butter (melted)
- 1 tsp. salt
- 1 tsp. chopped chives
- 1 tbsp. minced garlic

Step-by-Step Directions to Cook It:

1. Preheat the air fryer to 380^0F.
2. To prepare the butter mixture, add the lemon juice, salt, chives, garlic in a bowl. Mix until well combined.
3. To prepare the lobster tail, cut through the shell, and remove the meat. Rest the meat on top of the shell. Transfer to an air fryer basket. Spread the butter mixture over the meat.
4. Transfer to the air fryer and close the lid, set the time for 4 minutes. Open the air fryer and spread more butter on the lobster; allow to cook for another 4 minutes or until done.
5. Serve and enjoy.

Nutritional value per serving:

Calories: 120kcal, Fat: 12g, Carb: 1g, Proteins: 10g

Air Fryer Marinated Salmon

You will be surprised at how crusty and flaky the salmon is, especially after being cooked to perfection.
Prep time and cooking time: 30 minutes|
Serves: 4

Ingredients To Use:

- 4 salmon fillets
- 1/2 tbsp. minced garlic
- 6 tbsp. soy sauce
- 1 tbsp. brown sugar
- 1 green onion (finely chopped)
- 1/4 cup of Dijon mustard

Step-by-Step Directions to Cook It:

1. In a bowl, add all the ingredients and whisk until well combined. Pour the mixture over the salmon and refrigerate for 20 minutes.
2. Preheat the air fryer to 400^0F, transfer the salmon into a greased pan that fits into the air fryer. Place in the air fryer and close the lid, set the time for 12 minutes.
3. Remove from the air fryer, serve garnished with green onions, enjoy!

Nutritional value per serving:

Calories: 215kcal, Fat: 11g, Carb: 3g, Proteins: 34g

Hawaiian Salmon

The Hawaiian salmon recipe creates a colorful and vibrant dish that can be served as a romantic dinner.
Prep time and cooking time: 20 minutes|
Serves: 2

Ingredients To Use:

- 2 salmon fillets
- 2o oz. canned pineapple pieces and juice
- 1 tbsp. Balsamic vinegar
- 1/2 tsp. grated ginger

- 1 tsp. onion powder
- 2 tsp. garlic powder
- Salt and pepper to taste

Step-by-Step Directions to Cook It:

1. Preheat the air fryer to 350°F.
2. Season the fillets with salt, pepper, onion powder, garlic powder, and rub well. Transfer to a pan that fits into the air fryer; add the pineapple pieces, juice, ginger, and mix gently. Drizzle with vinegar and transfer into your air fryer; set the time for 10 minutes.
3. Serve and enjoy!

Nutritional value per serving:

Calories: 200kcal, Fat: 8g, Carb: 12g, Proteins: 20g

Chinese Cod

The Asian cod is a nice and tasty recipe that can be enjoyed with vegetable stir fry.
Prep time and cooking time: 20 minutes| Serves: 2

Ingredients To Use:

- 2 cod fillets
- 1 tbsp. soy sauce
- 1 tsp. peanuts (crushed)
- 1/2 tsp. ginger (grated)
- 2 tsp. garlic powder

Step-by-Step Directions to Cook It:

1. Preheat the air fryer to 390°F.
2. In a pan that fits into the air fryer, add all the ingredients, and toss gently. Transfer to the air fryer and close the lid. Set the time for 10 minutes.
3. Serve and enjoy!

Nutritional value per serving:

Calories: 234kcal, Fat: 10g, Carb: 12g, Proteins: 21g

Roasted Cod and Prosciutto

The roasted cod and prosciutto meal is creamy and fancy. Prepare on days when you wish to impress someone.
Prep time and cooking time: 20 minutes| Serves: 4

Ingredients To Use:

- 4 cod fillets
- 3 tbsp. prosciutto (chopped)
- 1 tbsp. chopped parsley
- 1 shallot, chopped
- 2 tbsp. lemon juice
- 2 garlic (pressed)
- 1 tsp. Dijon mustard
- 1/4 cup melted butter
- Salt and black pepper to taste

Step-by-Step Directions to Cook It:

1. Preheat the air fryer to 390°F.
2. In a bowl, mix all the ingredients except the fillets, whisk thoroughly. Season the fillets with salt and pepper. Spread the prosciutto mixture all over the fillets, transfer to the air fryer basket. Close the lid and set the time for 10 minutes.
3. Serve and enjoy!

Nutritional value per serving:

Calories: 200kcal, Fat: 4g, Carb: 6g, Proteins: 13g

Salmon and Chives Vinaigrette

The salmon and chives vinaigrette recipe is a game-changer with simple but delectable ingredients that combines with the fish's flavor to create something unique.
Prep time and cooking time: 22 minutes| Serves: 4

Ingredients To Use:

- 4 salmon fillets

- 3 tbsp. balsamic vinegar
- 2 tbsp. chopped dill
- 1/3 cup maple syrup
- 1 tbsp. olive oil
- 2 tbsp. chopped chives
- Salt and pepper to taste

Step-by-Step Directions to Cook It:

1. Preheat the air fryer to 350^0F.
2. Season the fish with salt, pepper, and oil. Transfer to the air fryer and close the lid. Set the time for 8 minutes, flip in between the cooking.
3. Meanwhile, place a pot over medium heat, add the vinegar, chives, maple syrup, and dill. Stir and cook for 3 minutes.
4. Serve the fish with chives vinaigrette on top, enjoy!

Nutritional value per serving:

Calories: 270kcal, Fat: 3g, Carb: 19g, Proteins: 21g

Prawn Wontons

The prawn wontons are crispy and crunchy and are better enjoyed with tomato ketchup. Prep time and cooking time: 35 minutes| Serves: 4

Ingredients To Use:

For Dough

- 5 tbsp. water
- 1-1/2 cup all-purpose flour
- 1/2 tsp. salt

For filling
- 2 cups minced prawns
- 2 tsp. soy sauce
- 2 tsp. vinegar
- 2 tsp. ginger-garlic paste
- 2 tbsp. oil

Step-by-Step Directions to Cook It:

1. Add all the dough ingredients to a bowl and mix. Knead the dough and cover with a plastic wrap. Place a saucepan over medium heat, add all the filling ingredients and cook for 10 minutes.
2. Preheat the air fryer to 200^0F.
3. Roll out doughs and place the filling in the center. Wrap the dough to cover the filling and pinch together at the edge.
4. Transfer the wontons to the air fryer basket and cover the lid. Set the time for 20 minutes.
5. Serve with ketchup or chili sauce.

Nutritional value per serving:

Calories: 281kcal, Fat: 6g, Carb: 18g, Proteins: 13g

Fish Fingers

Fish fingers are golden, super crispy, and crunchy on the outside but tender on the inside.

Prep time and cooking time: 1 hour 40 minutes| Serves: 2

Ingredients To Use:
- 1/2 lb. fish fillet cut into fingers
- 1 cup olive oil
- 1 tbsp. lemon juice
- 2 cups bread crumbs

For the marinade
- 3 tbsp. lemon juice
- 3 eggs
- 1-1/2 tbsp. ginger-garlic paste
- 2 tsp. ketchup
- 1-1/2 tsp. pepper powder
- 5 tbsp. cornflour
- 1 tsp. red chili flakes
- 2 tsp. salt

Step-by-Step Directions to Cook It:

1. Rub the lemon juice on the fingers and set aside. In a bowl, mix all the marinade

ingredients. Wash the fingers after 1 hour and pat dry. Transfer into the marinade bowl and leave for 15 minutes.
2. Preheat the air fryer to 160^{0}F.
3. Dip the fingers in breadcrumbs and transfer to the air fryer, close the lid, and set the time for 25 minutes.
4. Serve with ketchup or chili sauce.

Halibut and Sun-Dried Tomatoes Mix

The halibut and sun-dried tomatoes are flavourful and easily to be prepared in 20 minutes.
Prep time and cooking time: 20 minutes|
Serves: 2

Ingredients To Use:
- 2 halibut fillets
- 6 sun-dried tomatoes (chopped)
- 1/2 tsp. red pepper flakes
- 2 tsp. olive oil
- 2 small red onions (sliced)
- 9 black olives (sliced and pitted)
- 4 rosemary sprigs (chopped)
- 1 fennel bulb (sliced)
- 2 garlic cloves
- Salt and black pepper to taste

Step-by-Step Directions to Cook It:
1. Preheat the air fryer to 390^{0}F.
2. Place the fillets in a pan that fits into the air fryer, season with salt, pepper, and oil. Add the onion, tomatoes, rosemary, olives, pepper flakes, and rosemary. Close the lid and set the time for 10 minutes.
3. Serve and enjoy!

Fish and Couscous

The fish and couscous recipe is a tasty and healthy meal that will have your taste bud salivating.
Prep time and cooking time: 25 minutes|
Serves: 4

Ingredients To Use:
- 2-1/2 lb. sea bass (gutted)
- 2 red onions (chopped)
- 5 tsp. fennel seeds
- 1/4 cup toasted almonds (sliced)
- 2 fennel bulb (cored and sliced)
- 3/4 cup whole wheat couscous (cooked)
- Cooking spray
- Salt and black pepper to taste

Step-by-Step Directions to Cook It:
1. Preheat the air fryer to 350^{0}F.
2. Season the fish with salt and pepper, spray with cooking spray. Transfer to the air fryer cooking basket and close the lid. Set the time for 10 minutes.
3. Meanwhile, spray a saucepan with cooking oil and heat it over medium heat; add fennel seeds and cook for 1 minute. Add the fennel bulb, onion, almond, couscous, salt, and pepper. Cook for 2-3 minutes.
4. Serve the fish with the couscous.

Cod with Pearl Onions

The cod and pearl onion meal is rich creamy. The perfect comfort food on rainy days.

Prep time and cooking time: 25 minutes|
Serves: 2

Ingredients To Use:

- 2 cod fillets
- 1 tsp. dried thyme
- 8 oz. mushroom (sliced)
- 14 oz. pearl onion
- 1 tbsp. parsley
- Black pepper to taste

Step-by-Step Directions to Cook It:

1. Preheat the air fryer to 350^0F.
2. In a pan that fits into the air fryer, add all the ingredients, and toss gently. Transfer to the air fryer, close the lid, and set the time for 15 minutes.
3. Serve and enjoy!

Nutritional value per serving:

Calories: 270kcal, Fat: 10g, Carb: 12g, Proteins: 22g

Salmon and Avocado Salad

Salads are healthy and delicious, but when they are combined with air-fried salmon, the taste upgrades to a high new level.
Prep time and cooking time: 30 minutes|
Serves: 4

Ingredients To Use:

- 2 salmon fillets
- 2 tbsp. white wine vinegar
- 2 tbsp. olive oil
- 1/4 cup melted butter
- 4 oz. mushroom (slices)
- 1 0z. crumbled feta cheese
- 8 oz. lettuce leaves (chopped)
- 12 cherry tomato (halved)
- 5 cilantro sprigs (chopped)
- 1 avocado (peeled and cubed)
- 1 jalapeno pepper (chopped)
- Salt and black pepper to taste

Step-by-Step Directions to Cook It:

1. Preheat the air fryer to 350^0F.
2. Place the salmon on a lined baking sheet, brush with olive oil. Season with salt and pepper, Transfer to the air fryer, and cook for 15 minutes. Remove and keep warm.
3. Meanwhile, heat the butter in a pan over medium heat, add the mushroom, and cook for 2 minutes. Remove and transfer to a salad bowl; add the jalapeno, mushroom, cilantro, avocado, tomatoes, oil, salt, pepper, and vinegar. Toss well and sprinkle with cheese.
4. Serve the fish with the salad. Enjoy!

Nutritional value per serving:

Calories: 230kcal, Fat: 6g, Carb: 15g, Proteins: 9g

Salmon Fries

This recipe provides you with a flaky and crispy delicious fish that's irresistible. The herbs are well infused with the fish to created a flavored and tasty meal.
Prep time and cooking time: 20 minutes|
Serves: 4

Ingredients To Use:

- 1 lb. boneless salmon fillets
- 2 tsp. red chili flakes
- 2 cups breadcrumbs
- 2 tsp. oregano

For the marinade

- 4 tbsp. lemon juice
- 1-1/2 tbsp. ginger-garlic paste
- 4 eggs
- 1 tsp. red chili powder
- 2 tsp. salt
- 6 tbsp. cornflour
- 1 tsp. pepper powder

Step-by-Step Directions to Cook It:

1. In a bowl, mix all the marinade ingredients, add the salmon fillets and leave to marinate overnight.
2. Preheat the air fryer to 350^{0}F.
3. In a bowl, mix breadcrumbs, chili flakes and oregano, add the marinated fillets and mix. Transfer to the air fryer and cover with the lid, set the time for 15 minutes.
4. Serve and enjoy.

Nutritional value per serving:

Calories: 310kcal, Fat: 9g, Carb: 3g, Proteins: 17g

Salmon Fritters

Salmon fritter is a nice and delicious meal that can be enjoyed as lunch or dinner. It is crispy, delicious, and tasty.
Prep time and cooking time: 45 minutes| Serves: 4

Ingredients To Use:
- 1 lb. fileted salmon
- 2 tbsp. freshly chopped coriander leaves
- 2 tbsp. garam masala
- 3 green chili (finely chopped)
- 2 tsp. freshly chopped ginger
- 1-1/2 tbsp. lemon juice
- Salt and pepper to taste

Step-by-Step Directions to Cook It:
1. Preheat the air fryer to 160^{0}F.
2. In a food processor, add all the ingredients except the salmon. Pulse until it forms a smooth paste. Pour into a bowl and add the salmon, toss to coat.
3. Transfer to the air fryer, and close the lid. Set the time for 45 minutes.
4. Serve drizzled with lemon juice and enjoy!

Nutritional value per serving:

Calories: 271kcal, Fat: 9g, Carb: 6g, Proteins: 14g

Mustard Salmon

The mustard salmon will only take about 20 minutes to air fry, and it is absolutely delicious.
Prep time and cooking time: 20 minutes| Serves: 1

Ingredients To Use:
- 1 big salmon fillets
- 1 tbsp. coconut oil
- 1 tbsp. maple extract
- 2 tbsp. mustard
- Salt and pepper to taste
- Cooking spray

Step-by-Step Directions to Cook It:
1. Preheat the air fryer to 370^{0}F.
2. In a bowl, add the maple and mustard, whisk well. Season the fillet with salt, pepper, and oil. Brush the salmon with the maple mixture, spray with cooking spray. Transfer the mixture to the air fryer and set the time for 10 minutes.
3. Serve and enjoy!

Nutritional value per serving:

Calories: 300kcal, Fat: 7g, Carb: 16g, Proteins: 20g

Carp Fritters

The carp fritters is a nice and tasty recipe that will leave you craving for more.
Prep time and cooking time: 35 minutes| Serves: 4

Ingredients To Use:
- 10 carp fillets
- 3 eggs
- 3 onions chopped

- 1-1/2 tsp. salt
- 1-1/2 tbsp. ginger paste
- 1-1/2 tbsp. garlic paste
- 5 green chilies, freshly chopped
- 2 -1/2 tbsp. sesame seed
- 3 tsp. lemon juice
- 2 tsp. garam masala

Step-by-Step Directions to Cook It:

1. Preheat the air fryer to 160°F.
2. In a food processor, add all the ingredients except the filets and the eggs. Pulse until it forms a smooth paste. Pour into a bowl and add the filets, toss to coat. Beat the egg in a bowl, add salt.
3. Dip the coated fish in the egg, then in the sesame seeds, transfer to the air fryer, and close the lid. Set the time for 25 minutes.
4. Serve and enjoy!

Nutritional value per serving:

Calories: 312kcal, Fat: 9g, Carb: 12g, Proteins: 13g

Squid and Guacamole

Squid and guacamole may seem like a weird combination at first, but you won't feel the same after trying this recipe. The meat is tasty and delicious.

Prep time and cooking time: 16 minutes|

Serves: 2

Ingredients To Use:

- 2 medium squid, tentacles separated and tubes scored lengthwise
- Juice from 1 lime
- 1 tbsp. olive oil
- Salt and pepper to taste

For the Guacamole:

- Juice from 2 lime
- 2 avocados (pitted, cored, and chopped)
- 2 red chilies, chopped
- 1 tomato, chopped
- 1 tbsp. chopped coriander
- 1 red onion, chopped

Step-by-Step Directions to Cook It:

1. Preheat the air fryer to 360°F.
2. Season the squid with salt, pepper, and olive oil. Transfer to the air fryer basket and cook for 3 minutes per side. Remove and transfer to a bowl, drizzle with lime juice, and set aside.
3. Meanwhile, put the avocado in a bowl and mash, add the rest of the guacamole ingredients and mix well.
4. Serve the squid with the guacamole.

Nutritional value per serving:

Calories: 370kcal, Fat: 31g, Carb: 6g, Proteins: 20g

Chapter 4: Savory Beef

Beef stuffed Squash

Are you searching for a perfect squash recipe? Then you are in luck because this beef stuffed squash sets the pace for others. It is easy to prepare and takes less than 1 hour. Cook in batches and you will enjoy this delicious meal in no time.

Prep time and cooking time: 40 minutes| Serves: 2

Ingredients To Use:

- 1 lb. ground beef
- 1 tsp. dried oregano
- 1 spaghetti squash (pricked)
- 3 garlic cloves (minced)
- 28 oz. canned tomatoes (chopped)
- 1 Portobello mushroom (sliced)
- 1/2 tsp. dried thyme
- 1 green bell pepper (chopped)
- 1/4 tsp. cayenne pepper
- 1 yellow onion (diced)
- Salt and pepper to taste

Step-by-Step Directions to Cook It:

1. Preheat the air fryer to 350^{0}F, transfer the spaghetti squash into the air fryer, and cook for 20 minutes. Remove and transfer to the cutting board and cut into halves. Remove and discard the seeds.
2. Heat a pan over medium heat, add the beef, garlic, onions, mushroom, stir and cook until the meat is golden brown. Add the remaining ingredients except for the squash and allow them to cook for 10 minutes.
3. Stuff the squash with the beef mix and transfer into the air fryer; cook for 10 minutes at 360^{0}F.
4. Serve and enjoy.

Nutritional value per serving:

Calories: 260kcal, Fat: 7g, Carb: 14g, Proteins: 10g

Beef Casserole

This traditional beef stew recipe is easy to prepare and works perfectly when entertaining guests. The beef is tasty and tender.

Prep time and cooking time: 1 hour 15 minutes| Serves: 12

Ingredients To Use:

- 2 lb. beef
- 2 tsp. mustard
- 2 cups of grated mozzarella
- 1 tbsp. olive oil
- 2 cups. chopped eggplant
- 28 oz. canned tomatoes (chopped)
- 1 tsp. dried oregano
- 2 tsp. Worcestershire sauce
- 2 tbsp. chopped parsley
- 16 oz. tomato sauce
- Salt and pepper to taste

Step-by-Step Directions to Cook It:

1. Preheat the air fryer to 360^{0}F.
2. In a bowl, add eggplant, salt, pepper, and oil, mix to coat.
3. In a separate bowl, add beef, mustard, salt, pepper, and Worcestershire sauce, stir well. Pour the mixture into a pan that fits into your air fryer and spread evenly; add the eggplant mix and tomato sauce. Sprinkle with parsley and oregano.
4. Transfer to the air fryer and cook 35

minutes.

5. Serve and enjoy.

Nutritional value per serving:

Calories: 200kcal, Fat: 12g, Carb: 16g, Proteins: 15g

Burgundy Beef Mix

The burgundy beef mix is easy to prepare and extremely tasty.
Prep time and cooking time: 1hour 10 minutes| Serves: 7

Ingredients To Use:

- 2 lb. beef chuck roast, cut into smaller cubes
- 4 carrots (chopped)
- 1 cup of water
- 1 cup. beef stock
- 3 tbsp. almond flour
- 2 yellow onions (chopped)
- 1 tbsp. chopped thyme
- 2 celery ribs (chopped)
- 1/2 lb. mushroom (sliced)
- 15 oz. canned tomatoes(chopped)
- 1/2 tsp. mustard powder
- Salt and black pepper to taste

Step-by-Step Directions to Cook It:

1. Preheat the air fryer to 300°F.
2. Place a medium pot over high heat; add the meat and brown on all sides for 3-5 minutes. Add the tomato, carrot, onions, celery, mushroom, salt, pepper, mustard, stock, and thyme, stir.
3. In a bowl, add water and flour, stir. Add to the pot and transfer into the air fryer and cook for 1 hour.
4. Serve and enjoy.

Nutritional value per serving:

Calories: 275kcal, Fat: 13g, Carb: 17g, Proteins: 28g

Mexican Beef Mix

This recipe is like all traditional Mexican recipes; it's spicy and delicious.
Prep time and cooking time: 1hour 20 minutes| Serves: 8

Ingredients To Use:

- 2 lb. beef roast, cubes
- 2 green bell peppers (chopped)
- 6 garlic cloves (minced)
- 2 tbsp. olive oil
- 4 jalapenos (chopped)
- 2 yellow onions (diced)
- 1/2 cup of water
- 1 tsp. dried oregano
- 1 Habanero pepper (chopped)
- 2 tbsp. cilantro (chopped)
- 14 oz. canned tomatoes (chopped)
- 1/2 cup of black olive (pitted and chopped)
- 1 and 1/2 tsp. ground cumin
- Salt and pepper to taste

Step-by-Step Directions to Cook It:

1. Preheat the air fryer to 300°F.
2. In a pan, add all the ingredients and stir, transfer to the air fryer and cook for 1 hour 10 minutes.
3. Serve garnished with olives.

Nutritional value per serving:

Calories: 305kcal, Fat: 14g, Carb: 1825g, Proteins: g

Coffee Flavoured Steak

A defining feature of this dish is the ground coffee added to improve the flavor and aroma.
Prep time and cooking time: 25 minutes| Serves: 4

Ingredients To Use:

- 4 rib-eye steak

- 2 tbsp. garlic powder
- 2 tbsp. chili powder
- 1-1/2 tbsp. ground coffee
- 2 tbsp. onion powder
- 1/2 tbsp. sweet paprika
- Pinch of cayenne pepper
- 1/4 tsp. ground ginger
- Black pepper to taste
- 1/4 tsp. ground coriander

Step-by-Step Directions to Cook It:
1. Preheat the air fryer to 360°F.
2. In a bowl, mix all the ingredients except the steak and stir. Rub the steak thoroughly with the mixture.
3. Transfer to the air fryer and cook for 15 minutes.
4. Serve and enjoy.

Nutritional value per serving:

Calories: 160kcal, Fat: 10g, Carb: 14g, Proteins: 12g

Balsamic Beef

Balsamic beef is the perfect comfort food. It is always there to pick you up on rainy days and sunny ones.
Prep time and cooking time: 1hour 10 minutes| Serves: 6

Ingredients To Use:
- 1 medium beef roast
- 4 garlic cloves (pressed)
- 1 cup beef stock
- 1 tbsp. Worcestershire sauce
- 1 tbsp. soy sauce
- 1/2 cup balsamic vinegar
- 1 tbsp. honey

Step-by-Step Directions to Cook It:
1. Preheat the air fryer to 360°F.
2. In a pan, mix beef roast with vinegar, Worcestershire sauce, honey, garlic,

stock, and soy sauce. Transfer into the air fryer and cook for 1 hour.
3. Serve and enjoy!

Nutritional value per serving:

Calories: 311kcal, Fat: 12g, Carb: 20g, Proteins: 16g

Beef Medallion Mix

The beef mix is tender and juicy and can be prepared in no time—the perfect meal for a weeknight.
Prep time and cooking time: 2hours 10 minutes| Serves: 4

Ingredients To Use:
- 4 beef medallion
- 2 tbsp. lime juice
- 1 cup tomatoes (crushed)
- 2 tbsp. soy sauce
- 1 tsp. chili powder
- 1 tbsp. hot pepper
- 2 tsp. onion powder
- 2 tsp. onion powder
- Salt and black pepper to taste

Step-by-Step Directions to Cook It:
1. In a bowl, mix all the ingredients except the beef and whisk well. Arrange the beef in a pan, pour the sauce over the beef. Set aside for 2 hours.
2. Preheat the air fryer to 360°F.
3. Discard the tomato marinade, and transfer to the air fryer. Cook for 10 minutes.
4. Serve and enjoy!

Nutritional value per serving:

Calories: 230kcal, Fat: 4g, Carb: 13g, Proteins: 14g

Beef Kabobs

Beef kabobs are the perfect meal for a

summer gathering; the flavors and taste will leave your guest craving for more.

Prep time and cooking time: 20 minutes| Serves: 4

Ingredients To Use:

- 2 lb. sirloin steak (cut into medium sizes)
- 2 tbsp. chili powder
- 1 red onion (chopped)
- 1/4 cup olive oil
- 2 red peppers (chopped)
- 1/2 tbsp. ground cumin
- 2 tbsp. hot sauce
- Juice from 1 lime
- 1 zucchini (sliced)
- 1/4 cup of salsa
- Salt and pepper to taste

Step-by-Step Directions to Cook It:

1. Preheat the air fryer to 370^{0}F.
2. In a bowl, mix oil, salsa, hot sauce, cumin, lime juice, black pepper, and salt. Whisk thoroughly.
3. Arrange the meat, bell pepper, onions, and zucchini on a skewer, brush with salsa mix. Arrange in your air fryer and cook for 10 minutes.
4. Better enjoyed with salad at the side.

Nutritional value per serving:

Calories: 170kcal, Fat: 5g, Carb: 13g, Proteins: 16g

Mediterranean Steak Scallops

The flavored steak is served with the scallion, which serves as an excellent additive to the dish. A perfect meal to cook for a large crowd.

Prep time and cooking time: 25 minutes| Serves: 2

Ingredients To Use:

- 2 beef steaks
- 1/4 cup butter

- 1 tsp. lemon zest
- 4 garlic cloves, pressed
- 1 shallot, chopped
- 10 sea scallops
- 2 tbsp. chopped parsley
- 1/4 cup vegetable stock
- 2 tbsp. chopped basil
- 2 tbsp. lemon juice
- Salt and pepper to taste

Step-by-Step Directions to Cook It:

1. In a bowl, mix all the ingredients except the beef. Arrange the beef in a dish and pour the sauce over it. Leave to marinate for 2 hours.
2. Preheat the air fryer to 360^{0}F.
3. Discard the marinade and transfer beef to the air fryer, cook for 10 minutes.
4. Serve and enjoy with salad on the side.

Nutritional value per serving:

Calories: 150kcal, Fat: 2g, Carb: 14g, Proteins: 17g

Air Fryer Beef Steak

Air fryer beef steak is easy to prepare, and the final taste will leave you wanting for more. Juicy and delicious, enjoy with salad as a side.

Prep time and cooking time: 20 minutes| Serves: 4

Ingredients To Use:

- 2 lb. rib-eye steak
- 1 tbsp. olive oil
- Pepper and salt to taste

Step-by-Step Directions to Cook It:

1. Preheat the air fryer to 356^{0}F.
2. Season the beef on both sides with salt and pepper, rub with olive oil. Transfer into the air fryer and cook for 15 minutes (flip after 7 minutes).

3. Remove and allow the meat to rest for 3 minutes, carve, and serve. Enjoy!

Nutritional value per serving:

Calories: 233kcal, Fat: 19g, Carb: 2g, Proteins: 16g

Mushroom Meatloaf

This is the right recipe for recreating a juicy and tender meatloaf. It also tastes better when served with sauce.
Prep time and cooking time: 30 minutes|
Serves: 4

Ingredients To Use:
- 14 oz. lean ground beef
- 3 tbsp. breadcrumbs
- 1 chorizo sausage (finely chopped)
- 1 garlic clove (minced)
- 2 tbsp. freshly chopped cilantro
- 1 small onion (chopped)
- 1 egg
- 3 tbsp. olive oil
- 2 tbsp. freshly sliced mushroom
- Salt and pepper to taste

Step-by-Step Directions to Cook It:
1. Preheat the air fryer to 390^0F.
2. In a bowl, add all the ingredients except mushroom, mix until well combined. Pour the mixture into a bowl and level the surface with a spatula.
3. Arrange the mushroom on top and drizzle with oil. Transfer to the air fryer basket, close the lid of the air fryer. Set time to 25 minutes, open the air fryer, and remove the meatloaf. Allow to rest and serve.

Nutritional value per serving:

Calories: 284kcal, Fat: 7.9g, Carb: 46g, Proteins: 17.9g

Air Fried Steak Sandwich

One salient advantage of this recipe is that it can be prepared in less than 30 minutes; perfect for the morning rush.
Prep time and cooking time: 22 minutes|
Serves: 4

Ingredients To Use:
- 6 oz. sirloin steak cut into smaller pieces
- 8 medium-size cherry tomatoes (sliced)
- 1/2 tbsp. soy sauce
- 1 cup arugula, rinsed and dried
- 1/2 tbsp. of mustard powder
- 1 tbsp. bleu cheese (crumbled)
- 1 hoagie bun (sliced in half)

Step-by-Step Directions to Cook It:
1. Preheat the air fryer to 320^0F.
2. In a bowl, mix onion powder and soy sauce until thoroughly combined. Immerse the steak in the mixture for 1-2 minutes. Arrange the steak on a tin foil and transfer to the air fryer basket. Lay the hoagie-bun halves in the air fryer (crusty side up, soft-side down).
3. Close the air fryer lid and set time to 10 minutes; open the lid and flip the hoagie-buns (crusty side down, soft-side up). Sprinkle bleu cheese on the buns, close the air fryer and cook additional 6 minutes.
4. Open the air fryer lid, Remove the hoagie buns, arrange the steak, tomatoes, and arugula on the halved bun. Close with the other half, enjoy.

Nutritional value per serving:

Calories: 284kcal, Fat: 7.9g, Carb: 5.5g, Proteins: 17.9g

Carrot and Beef Cocktail Balls

This Carrot and Beef cocktail balls recipe is fragrant and flavor-packed.
Prep time and cooking time: 25 minutes|

55

Serves: 10

- 1 lb. ground beef
- 1 egg
- 1 red onion (chopped)
- 2 cloves garlic
- 1/2 tsp. dried oregano
- 1/2 tsp. Salt
- 1/2 tsp. dried rosemary (crushed)
- 1/2 tsp. dried basil
- 3/4 breadcrumbs
- 2 carrots (diced)
- 1/2 tsp. black pepper
- 1 cup plain flour

Step-by-Step Directions to Cook It:

1. Preheat the air fryer to 350°F.
2. Place the ground beef in a bowl, add onion, carrot, and garlic in a food processor. Pulse until smooth. Pour the mixture into the bowl containing the meat, add the remaining ingredient, and mix.
3. Shape the mixture into a ball and refrigerate for 30 minutes, remove and roll into the flour. Arrange in the air fryer and close the lid. Set time to 20 minutes, turning occasionally.
4. Serve and enjoy.

Nutritional value per serving:

Calories: 284kcal, Fat: 7.9g, Carb: 4.5g, Proteins: 23g

Beef Steak with Beans

This delicious and spicy recipe is best served and enjoyed with rice for maximum taste and aroma.

Prep time and cooking time: 15 minutes| Serves: 4

Ingredients To Use:

- 4 beef steak cut into strips
- 3/4 cup beef broth
- 1 cup green onions (chopped)
- 1/4 tsp. dried basil
- 1 can tomatoes (crushed)
- 1 red bell pepper (seed removed and thinly sliced)
- 1 can of cannellini beans
- 2 garlic cloves (minced)
- 1/2 tsp. sea salt
- 1/2 tsp. cayenne pepper
- Black pepper to taste

Step-by-Step Directions to Cook It:

1. Preheat the air fryer to 3900F.
2. In a pan that fits into the air fryer, add garlic, onions, steak. Close the air fryer and set the time to 10 minutes. Open the lid and stir in the remaining ingredients.
3. Cover and set time to 5 minutes, open the lid, and serve.
4. Enjoy!

Nutritional value per serving:

Calories: 275kcal, Fat: 7.5g, Carb: 4.3g, Proteins: 25g

Flavoured Rib Eye Steak

The name of the recipe says it all. You get a juicy and tender steak that just melts on your palate.

Prep time and cooking time: 30 minutes| Serves: 4

Ingredients To Use:

- 2lb. rib-eye steak
- 1 tbsp. olive oil
- Salt and black pepper to taste

Rub

- 2 tbsp. onion powder
- 1 tbsp. brown sugar
- 3 tbsp. sweet paprika
- 1 tbsp. grounded cumin
- 2 tbsp. garlic powder

- 1 tbsp. dried rosemary
- 2 tbsp. dried oregano

Step-by-Step Directions to Cook It:

1. Preheat the air fryer to 400⁰ F.
2. In a bowl, mix all the rub ingredients. Rub the steak on both sides with the mixture.
3. Season the steak with salt and pepper, and rub with olive oil.
4. Put in your air fryer and cook for 20 minutes (flip after 10minutes).
5. Remove the steak and allow it to sit for 5 minutes. Slice and enjoy with salad.

Nutritional value per serving:

Calories: 320kcal, Fat: 8g, Carb: 22g, Proteins: 21g

Chinese-Style Spicy and Herby Beef

The herbs and spices in this delightful Chinese recipe infuse the beef with great taste.
Prep time and cooking time: 45 minutes|
Serves: 4

Ingredients To Use:

- 1 lb. flank steak (cut into smaller)
- 3 tbsp. Shaoxing wine
- 1 tsp. fresh sage leaves (minced)
- 1/3 cup olive oil
- 3 cloves garlic (minced)
- 3 tsp. sesame oil
- 2 tbsp. tamari
- 1/8 tsp. xanthium
- 1 tsp. fresh rosemary, freshly minced
- 1 tsp. hot sauce
- 1/2 tsp. freshly cracked pepper

Step-by-Step Directions to Cook It:

1. Preheat the air fryer to 345⁰ F.
2. Warm oil in a pan over medium heat, add garlic, and sauté until fragrant. Add the

remaining ingredient and stir.
3. Transfer to the air fryer and set time to 18 minutes.
4. Serve and enjoy!

Nutritional value per serving:

Calories: 254kcal, Fat: 24g, Carb: 8g, Proteins: 21g

Filet Mignon Steak

With this recipe, you don't have to go to a restaurant to get your premium filet mignon.
Prep time and cooking time: 45 minutes|
Serves: 6

Ingredients To Use:

- 6 filet mignon steaks
- 1/2 cup heavy cream
- 2 tsp. freshly cracked peppercorn (mixed)
- 1/2 medium-size garlic bulb (peeled and pressed)
- 1-1/2 tbsp. apple cider
- 1-1/2 tsp. sea salt flakes
- A dash of hot sauce

Step-by-Step Directions to Cook It:

1. Preheat the air fryer to 385⁰ F.
2. Season the steak with peppercorn and salt flakes. Transfer to the air fryer basket. Cook for 24 minutes, turning halfway through the cooking time. Remove and set aside.
3. Place a saucepan over medium heat, add all the ingredients and whisk until it assumes a uniform consistency.
4. Serve the steak with the sauce.

Nutritional value per serving:

Calories: 452kcal, Fat: 32g, Carb: 8g, Proteins: 26g

Beef, Olives, and Tomatoes

Beef with olives and tomatoes is a rich and

creamy delicacy that will set your taste buds on a wild, beautiful dance. It is spicy and delicious with nice aroma.

Prep time and cooking time: 45 minutes| Serves: 4

Ingredients To Use:

- 2 lb. beef (cubed)
- 1 tbsp. smoked paprika
- 1 cup black olives (pitted and halved)
- 3 tbsp. olive oil
- 1 cup cherry tomatoes (halved)
- 1 tsp. ground coriander
- Salt and black pepper to taste

Step-by-Step Directions to Cook It:

1. Preheat the air fryer to 390^0 F.
2. In a pan that fits, mix all the ingredients, and transfer to the air fryer. Set time to 35 minutes.
3. Serve and enjoy!

Nutritional value per serving:

Calories: 291kcal, Fat: 12g, Carb: 19g, Proteins: 26g

Beef Schnitzel

The amazing recipe is tangy and delicious.
Prep time and cooking time: 55 minutes| Serves: 2

Ingredients To Use:

- 1 beef schnitzel cut into strips
- 2 tbsp. vegetable oil
- 1 whole lemon
- 2 oz. breadcrumbs
- 1 whole egg, whisked

Step-by-Step Directions to Cook It:

1. Preheat the air fryer to 356^0 F.
2. In a bowl, add breadcrumbs, vegetable oil, and mix. Dip the schnitzel into the egg, then into the breadcrumb mixture to coat. Transfer to the air fryer cooking

basket and set time for 12 minutes.
3. Drizzle with lemon juice and serve.

Nutritional value per serving:

Calories: 346kcal, Fat: 11g, Carb: 3g, Proteins: 33g

Beef Roast with Red Potatoes

Beef roast with red potatoes is a classic recipe that can be prepared for lunch or dinner.

Prep time and cooking time: 55 minutes| Serves: 3

Ingredients To Use:

- 4 lb. roast beef
- 3 lb. red potatoes halved
- 2 tbsp. olive oil
- 1/2 tsp. freshly chopped rosemary
- 1 tsp. dried thyme
- 1 tsp. salt
- 1/4 tsp. freshly ground black pepper
- Black pepper, olive oil, and salt for garnish.

Step-by-Step Directions to Cook It:

1. Preheat the air fryer to 360^0 F.
2. In a bowl, mix all the spices and set aside. Rub oil onto the beef and season with the spice mixture.
3. Transfer the beef to the air fryer cooking basket and set time to 20 minutes. Open the air fryer and flip the meats, add the potatoes, and season with pepper and oil. Cook for another 20 minutes.
4. Remove the steak and allow to rest; cook the potatoes for an additional 10 minutes at 400^0F.
5. Serve with the steak.

Nutritional value per serving:

Calories: 346kcal, Fat: 11g, Carb: 4g, Proteins: 32g

Sirloin steak with Cremini Mushroom Sauce

The sirloin steak is succulent and tender when coupled with the creamy and tasty cremini mushroom sauce. It has a taste you will never forget!
Prep time and cooking time: 40 minutes|
Serves: 5

Ingredients To Use:

- 2 lb. sirloin steak cut into 5 pieces
- 1 lb. cremini mushroom sliced
- 1/2 tsp3 dried rosemary
- 1 tsp3 mustard
- 1/4 tsp. dried thyme
- 1 cup sour cream
- 2 tbsp. butter
- 1/2 tsp. curry powder
- 1 tsp. cayenne pepper
- 1/2 tsp3 dried dill
- Salt and black pepper to taste

Step-by-Step Directions to Cook It:

1. Preheat the air fryer to 396^0 F.
2. Grease a baking pan with butter, add the steak, cayenne pepper, black pepper, salt, dill, rosemary, and thyme. Stir and transfer to the air fryer. Set time to 9 minutes.
3. Open the air fryer, stir in the remaining ingredients and cook for another 5-7 minutes.
4. Serve and enjoy!

Nutritional value per serving:
Calories: 349kcal, Fat: 12g, Carb: 4g, Proteins: 49g

Irish Whisky Steak

Try something new with this great recipe; the result will be the most unlike taste you've ever experienced.
Prep time and cooking time: 2hours 45 minutes | Serves: 6

Ingredients To Use:

- 2 lb. sirloin steak
- 2 tbsp. olive oil
- 1-1/2 tbsp. tamari sauce
- 2 tbsp. Irish whiskey
- 1/3 tsp. ground ginger
- 2 garlic cloves (minced)
- 1/3 tsp. cayenne pepper
- Fine sea salt to taste

Step-by-Step Directions to Cook It:

1. Preheat the air fryer to 395^0 F.
2. In a bowl, add all the ingredient except olive oil in a bowl, pour into a ziploc bag, and leave to marinate for 2 hours.
3. Remove and drizzle with olive oil, transfer to the air fryer basket and cook for 22 minutes, turning halfway through.
4. Serve and enjoy.

Nutritional value per serving:
Calories: 260kcal, Fat: 17g, Carb: 8g, Proteins: 35g

Chapter 5: Flavourful Lamb and Goat Recipes

Lamb Shanks and Carrots

This meal is tasty and delicious and can be prepared with readily available ingredients in your kitchen.

Prep time and cooking time: 55 minutes| Serves: 4

Ingredients To Use:

- 4 lamb shanks
- 2 tbsp. water
- 2 tbsp. paste
- 2 tbsp. olive oil
- 4 oz. red wine
- 6 carrots, chopped
- 1 tsp. oregano
- 1 tomato, chopped
- Salt and black pepper to taste

Step-by-Step Directions to Cook It:

1. Preheat the air fryer to 360^{0}F.
2. Season the lamb shank with salt, pepper, and rub with oil. Transfer to the air fryer and cook for 10 minutes.
3. In a pan that fits into your air fryer, add carrot and the remaining ingredients. Add the lamb. Stir and transfer into the air fryer, close the lid, and cook for 35 minutes.
4. Serve and enjoy!

Nutritional value per serving:

Calories: 321kcal, Fat: 16g, Carb: 14g, Proteins: 26g

Tasty Lamb Ribs

Tasty lamb ribs are a treat you will want to enjoy with friends and family. All the ingredients are well blended to create a flavourful dish.

Prep time and cooking time: 55 minutes| Serves: 8

Ingredients To Use:

- 8 lamb ribs
- 1 tbsp. chopped rosemary
- 2 carrots, chopped
- 3 tbsp. white flour
- 4 garlic cloves, minced
- 2 tbsp. olive oil
- 2 cups veggie stock
- Salt and black pepper to taste

Step-by-Step Directions to Cook It:

1. Preheat the air fryer to 360^{0}F.
2. Season the lamb ribs with salt, pepper, rub with olive oil and garlic. Transfer to the air fryer and cook 10 minutes.
3. In a dish that fits into your air fryer, mix stock with flour and whisk. Add rosemary, lamb ribs, and carrots. Transfer into the air fryer and cook for 30 minutes.
4. Serve and enjoy!

Nutritional value per serving:

Calories: 302kcal, Fat: 7g, Carb: 22g, Proteins: 25g

Provencal lamb

The Provencal lamb is a rich and delicious dish that can be prepared in no time at all. The potatoes enliven the rich taste of the meal.

Prep time and cooking time: 50 minutes | Serves: 2

Ingredients To Use:

- 1 lb. lamb rack
- 3 tbsp. olive oil, divided
- 2 medium boiled potatoes
- 2 garlic cloves, minced
- 2 tsp. chopped thyme
- 2 medium tomatoes, halved
- 1 tsp. chopped rosemary
- 1/3 cup. sliced shallots
- 2 tbsp. water
- Salt and pepper to taste

Step-by-Step Directions to Cook It:

1. Preheat the air fryer to 360°F.
2. In a bowl, add garlic, salt, thyme, rosemary, and pepper, mix until it forms a paste. Season the lamb with salt, pepper, and the paste. Heat oil in a pan that fits into your air fryer brown the lamb for 2 minutes. Remove and set aside, add the shallots and potatoes, cook for 5 minutes. Add the remaining ingredients with the lamb.
3. Transfer into the air fryer, cover the lid and cook for 25 minutes.
4. Serve and enjoy!

Nutritional value per serving:

Calories: 261kcal, Fat: 10g, Carb: 17g, Proteins: 16g

Lamb Casserole

Lamb casserole is one of the best comfort foods you will ever taste. Nothing can be compared to the aroma and the tender taste of the lamb.

Prep time and cooking time: 1 hour 15 minutes | Serves:8

Ingredients To Use:

- 2 lb. lamb
- 2 tsp. mustard
- 2 cups of grated mozzarella
- 1 tbsp. olive oil
- 2 cups. chopped eggplant
- 28 oz. canned tomatoes (chopped)
- 1 tsp. dried oregano
- 2 tsp. Worcestershire sauce
- 2 tbsp. chopped parsley
- 16 oz. tomato sauce
- Salt and pepper to taste

Step-by-Step Directions to Cook It:

1. Preheat the air fryer to 360°F.
2. In a bowl, add eggplant, salt, pepper, and oil, mix to coat.
3. In another bowl, add lamb, mustard, salt, pepper, and Worcestershire sauce, stir well. Pour the mixture into a pan that fits into your air fryer and spread evenly; add the eggplant mix and tomato sauce. Sprinkle with parsley and oregano.
4. Transfer to the air fryer and cook 35 minutes.
5. Serve and enjoy!

Nutritional value per serving:

Calories: 210kcal, Fat: 10g, Carb: 14g, Proteins: 18g

Mediterranean Lamb Meatballs

Mediterranean dishes are always a delight, but these juicy and succulent meatballs have it all. It can be served as a main course meal or side dish.

Prep time and cooking time: 1 hour | Serves: 4

Ingredients To Use:

- 1 lb. ground lamb
- 3/4 cup breadcrumbs
- 1-1/2 tbsp. kosher salt
- 1-1/2 tbsp. Italian seasoning

For the tomato sauce:

- 5 cloves garlic
- 4 cups. water
- 1 onion, minced
- 1 tsp. cumin
- 5 cloves garlic, minced
- 3 red chilies, chopped
- 28 oz. can of crushed tomatoes
- 1 tbsp. dried parsley
- Salt and black pepper to taste
- Greek yogurt for toppings

Step-by-Step Directions to Cook It:

1. Preheat the air fryer to 360^{0}F.
2. In a bowl, add all the meatball ingredients and mix thoroughly. Scoop into a ball. In a pan that fits into the air fryer, heat oil on medium heat. Add the meatballs and brown for 5 minutes.
3. In a bowl, mix all the sauce ingredients, pour over the meatballs, and transfer into your air fryer. Close the lid and set time to 30 minutes.
4. Serve and enjoy!

Nutritional value per serving:

Calories: 185kcal, Fat: 11g, Carb: 8g, Proteins: 14g

Greek Lamb Chop

The super tender and flavourful Greek lamb chop comes together in no time at all. The herbs and spice are well infused in the lamb to create a juicy taste.
Prep time and cooking time: 35 minutes|
Serves: 4

Ingredients To Use:
- 8 loin lamb chops
- 2 tbsp. olive oil
- 1 tsp. oregano
- 4 tbsp. grainy mustard
- 1 tsp. thyme
- Salt and pepper

Step-by-Step Directions to Cook It:

1. Preheat the air fryer to 360^{0}F.
2. In a bowl, mix oil with oregano, mustard, and thyme. Season the lamb chops with salt and pepper, brush with the mustard mixture. Allow to rest for a few minutes, transfer to the air fryer, and cook for 20 minutes.
3. Serve and enjoy with sauce or dip.

Nutritional value per serving:

Calories: 324kcal, Fat: 7g, Carb: 1g, Proteins: 35g

Lamb Chops with Balsamic Glaze

Your tongue will appreciate the tender and juicy lamb chops coupled with the sweet taste of the balsamic glaze. Easy to prepare for everyday cooking.
Prep time and cooking time: 40 minutes |
Serves: 4

Ingredients To Use:
- 8 loin lamb chops
- 2 tbsp. olive oil
- 1 tsp. pepper
- 2 tbsp. minced garlic
- 1/4 cup bourbon
- 1/2 cup brown sugar
- 1 tsp. salt
- 1/4 tsp. cayenne pepper
- 1/2 cup balsamic vinegar
- 1 tbsp. melted butter

Step-by-Step Directions to Cook It:

1. Preheat the air fryer to 360^{0}F.
2. Season the lamb chops with salt, pepper, and rub with oil. Transfer to the air fryer and cook for 5 minutes. Remove and set aside.
3. In a pan that fits into the air fryer, heat oil on medium heat. Add garlic and cook until fragrant. Add the remaining

ingredients with the lamb and cook for 20 minutes.

4. Serve and enjoy!

Nutritional value per serving:

Calories: 301kcal, Fat: 10g, Carb: 21g, Proteins: 12g

Air fryer Lamb rack

The air fryer lamb rack is a super tender and delicious dish that couldn't be any easier. It can be prepared in 30 minutes and is perfect for the ideal dinner.

Prep time and cooking time: 30 minutes | Serves: 4

Ingredients To Use:

- 2 rack of lamb
- 1 tbsp. minced rosemary
- 2 garlic cloves, pressed
- 1/2 cup Dijon mustard
- Salt and pepper to taste

Step-by-Step Directions to Cook It:

1. Preheat the air fryer to 360^0F.
2. Rinse the lamb rack and pat dry, season with salt and pepper, set aside. In a bowl, add garlic, rosemary, and mustard, mix well. Rub the lamb with the mixture and transfer to the air fryer basket. set time to 10 minutes.
3. Serve and enjoy!

Nutritional value per serving:

Calories: 321kcal, Fat: 12g, Carb: 1g, Proteins: 21g

Lamb Chops with Horseradish Sauce

Lamb chops with horseradish sauce are the perfect meal to entertain a special visitor. It is easy to prepare, flavourful, and tasty with the sauce.

Prep time and cooking time: 55 minutes | Serves: 2

Ingredients To Use:

- 8 loins lamb chops
- 1 tsp. black pepper
- 2 tbsp. vegetable oil
- 2 cloves garlic, minced
- 1 tsp. salt

Horseradish sauce:

- 1-1/2 tbsp. prepared horseradish
- 1/2 cup. mayonnaise
- 1 tbsp. Dijon mustard
- 2 tsp. sugar

Step-by-Step Directions to Cook It:

1. Preheat the air fryer to 360^0F.
2. season the lamb with salt, pepper, and rub with oil. Leave to marinate for 15 minutes. In a bowl, add horseradish, mayonnaise, sugar, and mustard. Stir well and half the sauce. Dip the lamb chops in the sauce, transfer to the air fryer, and set time to 15 minutes. Increase the temperature to 390^0F, cook for additional 5 minutes, flipping halfway.
3. Serve and enjoy with the sauce!

Nutritional value per serving:

Calories: 321kcal, Fat: 24g, Carb: 4g, Proteins: 21g

Lamb Roast and potatoes

Lamb roast and potatoes are a meal you will always like to prepare. The meat is tender and juicy combined with potatoes and spice, simply delicious.

Prep time and cooking time: 55 minutes | Serves: 6

Ingredients To Use:

- 4 lb. lamb roast

- 6 potatoes, halved
- 1 spring rosemary
- 4 bay leaves
- 1/2 cup lamb stock
- 3 garlic cloves, minced
- Salt and black pepper to taste

Step-by-Step Directions to Cook It:

1. Preheat the air fryer to 360°F.
2. Add the potatoes to a bowl that fits into the air fryer, add the remaining ingredients, and transfer into the air fryer. Set time to 45 minutes.
3. Serve and enjoy!

Nutritional value per serving:

Calories: 273kcal, Fat: 4g, Carb: 24g, Proteins: 28g

Spicy lamb Stew with Chickpeas

This tasty and flavourful meal is spicy, warm, and the perfect comfort food for winter. This hearty meal is well seasoned as well as spiced.

Prep time and cooking time: 50 minutes| Serves: 4

Ingredients To Use:

- 1 lb. lamb stew meat
- 2 tbsp. vegetable oil divided
- 2 tbsp. lemon juice
- 1 cup dried chickpeas, soaked overnight
- 1 tbsp. minced garlic
- 1-1/2 tsp. salt
- 1-1/2 tsp. ground cumin
- 1 tsp. ground cinnamon
- 1 tsp. ground coriander
- 1 can (14 oz.) can tomatoes
- 1 tsp. ground turmeric
- 1/2 cup. chopped dried apricot
- 1/4 tsp. black pepper
- 1/4 cup of freshly chopped parsley
- 1 large onion, chopped

- 1-1/2 cups chicken broth
- 1 tbsp. honey
- Hot cooked couscous

Step-by-Step Directions to Cook It:

1. Drain the chickpea. In a pan that fits into the air fryer, add the meat. Brown for 15 minutes, remove and set aside. Add the remaining oil, garlic, onions, and cook until soft.
2. Stir in the remaining ingredients and transfer to the air fryer. Cover with the lid and set time to 30 minutes.
3. Serve and enjoy!

Nutritional value per serving:

Calories: 452kcal, Fat: 13g, Carb: 5g, Proteins: 21g

Lamb Stew With Almond and Apricots

Lamb stew with almond and apricot is a classic example of sweet and savory flavor. Popularly eaten in north Africa, enjoy with fresh juice.

Prep time and cooking time: 1hour 15 minutes| Serves: 6

Ingredients To Use:

- 2 lb. lamb shoulder, trimmed and cut into cubes
- 1 tsp. cinnamon
- 1 tsp. freshly cracked black pepper
- 1 tsp. ginger
- 1/4 tsp. ground coriander
- 1 tsp. ground ginger
- 1/2 cup of water
- 1/4 tsp. cardamom
- 1/4 tsp. cayenne
- 1 stick of unsalted butter
- 2 cinnamon stick
- 1 cup. chicken stock

- 1/2 cup. chopped parsley
- 2 tbsp. lemon juice
- 2 medium onion, chopped
- 1-1/2 cup. apricot, chopped
- 1/3 cup. honey
- 1-1/2 cup. almond

Step-by-Step Directions to Cook It:

1. In a bowl, add ginger, coriander, cinnamon, cardamom, pepper, cayenne, water, and mix well. Add the meat and toss to coat; leave to marinate overnight in the refrigerator.
2. Preheat the air fryer to 300^{0}F.
3. Heat oil in a pan over medium heat, add onions, garlic, cinnamon sticks, and cook until fragrant and translucent. Add the meat, including the marinade and stock. Transfer to the air fryer and cook for 50 minutes.
4. Open the lid and stir in the remaining ingredients, cover with the lid and cook for an additional 20 minutes.
5. Serve and enjoy!

Nutritional value per serving:

Calories: 467kcal, Fat: 13g, Carb: 24g, Proteins: 36g

Irish Lamb Stew with Bacon

Irish lamb stew and bacon is one hearty meal you will always like to have for dinner. It is also a great meal to consume the next day as it allows the flavors to infuse the lamb.
Prep time and cooking time: 2 hours 30 minutes| Serves: 6

Ingredients To Use:

- 1 lb. lamb shoulder
- 1/2 cup. water
- 1-1/2 cup. bacon
- 2 cup chicken stock
- 1/2 cup. plain flour

- 2 onions, finely chopped
- 1 tsp. dried thyme
- 1/2 cup. water
- 2 tsp. white sugar
- 2 cups. chopped carrots
- 1 cup. white wine
- 2 bay leaves
- 3 potatoes
- Salt and black pepper to taste

Step-by-Step Directions to Cook It:

1. Preheat the air fryer to 360^{0}F.
2. heat oil in a pan, add bacon and cook until crispy. In a bowl, add flour, salt, pepper, lamb. Toss to coat, add to the oil, and brown for a few minutes. Remove from heat.
3. Add garlic and onion and cook until fragrant; stir in the remaining ingredients. Transfer to the air fryer, cover with the lid and cook for 1 ½ hour.
4. Serve and Enjoy!

Nutritional value per serving:

Calories: 456kcal, Fat: 24g, Carb: 23g, Proteins: 43g

Basque Lamb Stew

This particular dish is a native of Spain, and a spicy and delicious meal that you will love. It is a stew perfect for winter.
Prep time and cooking time: 2 hours | Serves: 4

Ingredients To Use:

- 1 lb. lamb shoulder, cut into smaller pieces
- 1 tbsp. dried rosemary
- 1 onion, chopped
- 1/2 tsp. red chili flakes
- 6 cloves garlic, minced
- 1/2 cup. white wine
- 3 roasted red bell pepper, cut into thin

strips
- 2 tbsp. freshly chopped coriander
- 2 tbsp. olive oil
- 1 cup. vegetable stock
- 1 cup. red wine
- 1 bay leaf
- Salt and black pepper

Step-by-Step Directions to Cook It:

1. In a bowl, combine rosemary, white wine, and garlic, add the lamb and mix well. Leave to marinate overnight. Drain the meat and pat dry with paper towels.
2. Preheat the air fryer to 360⁰F, in a pan that fits into the air fryer, heat oil, and brown the meat for 1o minutes. Remove from the pan and add onions and garlic. Cook until soft and fragrant.
3. Stir in the remaining ingredients and transfer to the air fryer. Close the lid and set time to 1 hour.
4. Serve and enjoy!

Nutritional value per serving:

Calories: 523kcal, Fat: 23g, Carb: 16g, Proteins: 31g

Spicy Lamb Stew

The spicy lamb stew is a combination of flavors that you won't be able to resist.
Prep time and cooking time: 95 minutes| Serves:6

Ingredients To Use:
- 2 lb. boneless lamb shoulder
- Salt and black pepper to taste
- 1/4 cup all-purpose flour
- Juice of 1/2 lemon
- 1 tbsp. olive oil
- 1 medium onion, chopped
- 1/2 tsp. ground cumin
- 1 cup chicken stock
- 1/2 tsp. ground ginger

- 2 cloves garlic, minced
- 1/4 tsp. ground cinnamon
- 1 medium carrot, peeled and chopped
- 1 (14.5-ounce) can. Diced tomatoes

Step-by-Step Directions to Cook It:

1. Trim the lamb and season with salt and pepper; toss with the flour. Preheat the air fryer to 360⁰F.
2. heat oil in a pan, add the lamb and cook until brown on all sides. Toss to coat, add to the oil, and brown for a few minutes. Remove from heat.
3. Add garlic and onion and cook until fragrant; stir in the remaining ingredients. Transfer to the air fryer, cover with the lid and cook for 1-1/2 hour.
4. Serve and Enjoy!

Nutritional value per serving:

Calories: 527kcal, Fat: 30g, Carb: 26g, Proteins: 37g

Mutton Couscous

Mutton couscous is just like pork couscous, except it tastes better and has more combinations of flavors.
Prep time and cooking time: 45 minutes| Serves: 6

Ingredients To Use:
- 2 lb. lamb loin
- 3/4 cup. chicken stock
- 2 tbsp. olive oil
- 2 cups cooked couscous
- 1/2 tbsp. sweet paprika
- 1/2 tbsp. garlic powder
- 1 tsp. dried basil
- 1/4 tsp. dried marjoram
- 2 and 1/4 tsp. dried sage
- 1 tsp. oregano
- Salt and black pepper to taste

Step-by-Step Directions to Cook It:

1. Preheat the air fryer to 370°F.
2. In a bowl, add all the ingredients except the couscous, add the lamb, and leave to marinate for 1hour. Pour in a pan that fits into the air fryer.
3. Transfer to the air fryer, cook for 35 minutes.
4. Serve with couscous, enjoy!

Nutritional value per serving:

Calories: 326kcal, Fat: 12g, Carb: 9g, Proteins: 27g

Lamb with Beer Sauce

Lamb with beer sauce is a combination of flavor that you won't be forgetting anytime soon.

Prep time and cooking time: 60 minutes| Serves: 4

Ingredients To Use:
- 4 lb. lamb, cut into smaller piece
- 1 portobello mushroom, dried
- 1 onion, chopped
- 1 cup. chicken stock
- 1/4 cup tomato paste
- 6 thyme sprigs, chopped
- 1 cup dark beer
- Salt and pepper to taste

Step-by-Step Directions to Cook It:
1. Preheat the air fryer to 350°F.
2. Heat oil in a pan over medium heat, add garlic, green onions, and ginger, stir and cook for 1 minute.
3. Add the rib and the remaining ingredients, transfer to the air fryer and cook for 35 minutes.
4. Serve and enjoy.

Nutritional value per serving:

Calories: 321kcal, Fat: 12g, Carb: 20g, Proteins: 14g

Lamb with Onion Sauce

Lamb with onion sauce is creamy, juicy, and tasty. The perfect meal for a weeknight dinner.

Prep time and cooking time: 2 hours 10 minutes| Serves: 6

Ingredients To Use:
- 4 lb. lamb brisket
- 8 earl greys teabags
- 4 cups of water
- 1 lb. yellow onion, chopped
- 1 lb. carrot, chopped
- Salt and black pepper to taste
- 1/2 lb. celery, chopped

For sauce:
- 1 oz. garlic, minced
- 16 oz. canned tomatoes, chopped
- 4 oz. vegetable oil
- 1 cup white vinegar
- 1 lb. sweet onion, chopped
- 1 cup. white vinegar
- 1/2 lb. celery, chopped
- 8 earl grey tea bags

Step-by-Step Directions to Cook It:
1. Preheat the air fryer to 300°F.
2. In a pan that fits into the air fryer, add water, carrot, onion, celery, salt, and pepper. Bring to a boil over medium heat. Add the lamb and transfer to the air fryer and cook for 1 hour 30 minutes.
3. Meanwhile, for the sauce, heat oil in a pan over medium heat, add onion, celery, and sauce ingredients. Cook for 10 minutes.
4. Serve the lamb with the sauce.

Nutritional value per serving:

Calories: 400kcal, Fat: 12g, Carb: 28g, Proteins: 31g

Lamb Kabobs

Lamb kabob is just like its beef counterpart; however, they differ in taste because the lamb comes with its juicy flavor.
Prep time and cooking time: 20 minutes|
Serves: 4

Ingredients To Use:

- 2 lb. lamb steak (cut into medium sizes)
- 2 tbsp. chili powder
- 1 red onion (chopped)
- 1/4 cup olive oil
- 2 red peppers (chopped)
- 1/2 tbsp. ground cumin
- 2 tbsp. hot sauce
- Juice from 1 lime
- 1 zucchini (sliced)
- 1/4 cup of salsa
- Salt and pepper to taste

Step-by-Step Directions to Cook It:

1. Preheat the air fryer to Preheat the air fryer to 370^0F.
2. In a bowl, mix oil, salsa, hot sauce, cumin, lime juice, black pepper, and salt. Whisk thoroughly.
3. Arrange the meat, bell pepper, onions, and Zucchini on a skewer, brush with salsa mix. Arrange in your air fryer and cook for 10 minutes.
4. Better enjoyed with salad at the side.

Nutritional value per serving:

Calories: 170kcal, Fat: 5g, Carb: 13g, Proteins: 16g

Lamb Rack with wine sauce

The lamb is delicious and easy to prepare; the flavor, herbs, and spice create a wonderful dish.
Prep time and cooking time: 55 minutes|
Serves: 6

Ingredients To Use:

- 2 lb. lamb rack
- 3 carrot (chopped)
- 3 oz. red wine
- 1/2 tsp. smoked paprika
- 5 potatoes chopped
- 1/2 tsp. salt
- 1 yellow onion (chopped)
- 4 garlic clove (pressed)
- 17 oz. chicken stock
- 1/2 tsp. chicken salt

Step-by-Step Directions to Cook It:

1. Preheat the air fryer to 360^0F.
2. In a bowl, add salt, paprika, and chicken salt, stir. Rub the lamb with the mixture and transfer to a pan that will fit into the air dryer.
3. Add the remaining ingredients and cook for 45 minutes.
4. Enjoy and serve.

Nutritional value per serving:

Calories: 314kcal, Fat: 21g, Carb: 18g, Proteins: 36g

Mutton fries

Mutton fries are crispy as well as crusty; enjoy with ketchup or as a side dish.
Prep time and cooking time: 20 minutes|
Serves: 4

Ingredients To Use:

- 1 lb. boneless mutton (cut into fingers)
- 2 tsp. red chili flakes
- 2 tsp. oregano
- 2 cups dry breadcrumbs

For the Marinade:

- 4 tbsp. lemon juice
- 6 tbsp. cornflour
- 1-1/2 tbsp. ginger-garlic paste
- 1 tsp. red chili powder

- 4 eggs
- 2 tsp. salt
- 1 tsp. pepper powder

Step-by-Step Directions to Cook It:

1. In a bowl, add all the marinade ingredients and mix. Add the mutton fingers and leave to marinate overnight.
2. Preheat the air fryer to 160⁰F.
3. In a bowl, mix oregano with breadcrumbs and red chili flakes. Dip the fingers in the breadcrumb mixture and transfer to the air fryer. Close the lid and cook for 15 minutes.
4. Serve and enjoy!

Nutritional value per serving:

Calories: 432kcal, Fat: 13g, Carb: 15g, Proteins: 31g

Tasty Mutton Chops

This is a good option if lamb and beef are not available. It is tender, moist, and juicy, a good choice for weeknight dinner.
Prep time and cooking time: 35 minutes | Serves: 4

Ingredients To Use:

- 8 loin mutton chops
- 2 tbsp. olive oil
- 1 tsp. oregano
- 1 tsp. coriander
- 1 tsp. cumin
- 4 tbsp. grainy mustard
- 1 tsp. thyme
- Salt and pepper

Step-by-Step Directions to Cook It:

1. Preheat the air fryer to 350⁰F.
2. In a bowl, mix all the ingredients. Add the mutton chops and toss to coat.
3. Transfer to the air fryer and cook for 10 minutes.

4. Serve and enjoy!

Nutritional value per serving:

Calories: 231kcal, Fat: 7g, Carb: 6g, Proteins: 23g

Burgundy Lamb Shanks

This nice and tasty dish has it all, from aroma to taste. Enjoy with a glass of wine!
Prep time and cooking time: 1 hour 10 minutes | Serves: 6

Ingredients To Use:

- 2 lb. lamb roast, cut into smaller cubes
- 4 carrots (chopped)
- 1 cup of water
- 1 cup. beef stock
- 3 tbsp. almond flour
- 2 yellow onions (chopped)
- 1 tbsp. chopped thyme
- 2 celery ribs (chopped)
- 1/2 lb. mushroom (sliced)
- 15 oz. canned tomatoes(chopped)
- 1/2 tsp. mustard powder
- Salt and black pepper to taste

Step-by-Step Directions to Cook It:

1. Preheat the air fryer to 300⁰F.
2. Place a medium pot over high heat; add the meat and brown on all sides for 3-5 minutes. Add the tomato, carrot, onions, celery, mushroom, salt, pepper, mustard, stock, and thyme, stir.
3. In a bowl, add water and flour, stir. Add to the pot and transfer into the air fryer, cook for 1 hour.
4. Serve and enjoy.

Nutritional value per serving:

Calories: 275kcal, Fat: 13g, Carb: 17g, Proteins: 28g

Mutton stew

This recipe will create one big hearty meal that will lift your spirit. Also, it is very easy to prepare.

Prep time and cooking time: 95 minutes|
Serves: 4

Ingredients To Use:

- 2 lb. mutton, cut into cubes
- 1 tsp. cinnamon
- 1/4 tsp. cayenne
- 1 tsp. freshly cracked black pepper
- 1 tsp. ginger
- 1/4 tsp. ground coriander
- 1 tsp. ground ginger
- 1/2 cup of water
- 1/4 tsp. cardamom
- 1 stick of unsalted butter
- 2 cinnamon stick
- 1 cup. chicken stock
- 1/2 cup. chopped parsley
- 2 tbsp. lemon juice
- 2 medium onion, chopped

Step-by-Step Directions to Cook It:

1. In a bowl, add ginger, coriander, cinnamon, cardamom, pepper, cayenne, water, and mix well. Add the meat and toss to coat; leave to marinate overnight in the refrigerator.
2. Preheat the air fryer to 300°F.
3. Heat oil in a pan over medium heat, add onions, garlic, cinnamon sticks, and cook until fragrant and translucent. Add the meat, including the marinade and stock. Transfer to the air fryer and cook for 50 minutes.
4. Open the lid and stir in the remaining ingredients, cover with the lid and cook for an additional 20 minutes.
5. Serve and enjoy!

Nutritional value per serving:

Calories: 451kcal, Fat: 10g, Carb: 18g, Proteins: 38g

Herb Crusted Lamb Schnitzel

Lamb schnitzel is crispy and crusty on the outside but tasty and juicy on the inside. This nutritious meal is perfect for a dinner date, enjoy with a glass of wine.

Prep time and cooking time: 20 minutes|
Serves: 4

Ingredients To Use:

- 4 lamb schnitzel cut into strips
- 2 tbsp. melted butter
- 1 whole lemon
- 2 oz. breadcrumbs
- 1 whole egg, whisked
- 1/2 cup grated parmesan
- 2 tbsp. chopped fresh oregano
- Salt and pepper to taste

Step-by-Step Directions to Cook It:

1. Preheat the air fryer to 356° F.
2. In a bowl, add breadcrumbs, vegetable oil, cheese, oregano, and mix. Dip the schnitzel into the egg, then into the breadcrumb mixture to coat. Transfer to the air fryer cooking basket and set time for 12 minutes.
3. Drizzle with lemon juice and serve.

Nutritional value per serving:

Calories: 248kcal, Fat: 16g, Carb: 21g, Proteins: 36g

Air Fryer Lamb Chops

Air fryer Lamb chops is a simple but elegant meal. Ideal for serving during summer picnic or gathering. So tasty!

Prep time and cooking time: 30 minutes|
Serves: 8

Ingredients To Use:

- 16 lamb loin, cut into smaller piece

- 2 tbsp. lemon juice
- 4 sprigs rosemary
- 4 cloves garlic, minced
- 1 tbsp. lemon zest
- 1 tbsp. olive oil
- Salt and pepper to taste

Step-by-Step Directions to Cook It:

1. In a Ziploc bag, add all the ingredients with the lamb and leave to marinate in the refrigerator for 1 hour.
2. Preheat the air fryer to 360^0F, remove the marinade and transfer to the air fryer basket. Cover the lid and set time to 20 minutes, flipping halfway.
3. Serve and enjoy with any sauce of choice.

Nutritional value per serving:

Calories: 342kcal, Fat: 5g, Carb: 2g, Proteins: 37g

Greek Lamb Burger with Tzatziki Sauce

This delicious recipe is made of lamb seasoned with herb and spice and topped with the savory tzatziki sauce.

Prep time and cooking time: 30 minutes|

Serves: 4

Ingredients To Use:

- 1.5 lb. ground lamb
- 1 cup tzatziki sauce
- 1 tsp. oregano
- 1/2 head lettuce
- 1/3 cup. crumbled feta cheese
- 4 buns
- 1 medium tomato
- Salt and pepper to taste

Step-by-Step Directions to Cook It:

1. Preheat the air fryer to 375^0F.
2. In a bowl, add lamb, cheese, pepper, and oregano, combine thoroughly. Form into 6 patties sprinkle with salt and pepper. Spray with cooking oil and transfer to the air fryer basket. Close the lid and set time to 10 minutes turning halfway through.
3. Arrange the burger on the buns with lettuce, tomatoes, top with tzatziki sauce.
4. Enjoy!

Nutritional value per serving:

Calories: 340kcal, Fat: 10g, Carb: 23g, Proteins: 28g

Chapter 6: Mouth-watering Pork Recipes

Pork Chops and Green Beans

Pork chops and green beans combine both flavors and nutrients in one plate.
Prep time and cooking time: 25 minutes|
Serves: 4

Ingredients To Use:

- 4 pork chops
- 3 garlic cloves, minced
- 1 tbsp. chopped sage
- 16 oz. green beans
- 2 tbsp. chopped parsley
- 2 tbsp. olive oil
- Salt and black pepper to taste

Step-by-Step Directions to Cook It:

1. Preheat the air fryer to 360^0F. In a pan that fits into the air fryer, add all the ingredients and mix. Add the pork and mix well.
2. Transfer to the air fryer and set time to 15 minutes.
3. Serve and enjoy!

Nutritional value per serving:

Calories: 261kcal, Fat: 7g, Carb: 17g, Proteins: 20g

Pork Stew

Who doesn't love a steamed bowl of stew, with flavors and aromas that can't be easily forgotten.
Prep time and cooking time: 47 minutes|
Serves: 4

Ingredients To Use:

- 2 lb. pork meat, cubed
- 2 zucchinis, cubed

- 1/2 tsp. smoked paprika
- 1 eggplant, cubed
- 1 tbsp. cilantro, chopped
- 1/2 cup beef stock
- Salt and black pepper to taste

Step-by-Step Directions to Cook It:

1. Preheat the air fryer to 370^0F.
2. In a pan that fits into the air fryer, add all the ingredients with the beef. Mix well and transfer into the air fryer, set time to 30 minutes.
3. Serve and enjoy!

Nutritional value per serving:

Calories: 245kcal, Fat: 12g, Carb: 5g, Proteins: 14g

Pork Taquitos

Air frying is a healthy way of cooking this recipe. The pork tortilla can easily be available within 15 minutes, perfect for a stress-free lunch.
Prep time and cooking time: 15 minutes|
Serves: 10

Ingredients To Use:

- 3 cups cooked shredded pork
- 2-1/2 cup. Mozzarella cheese
- Juice of 1 lime
- 1o small tortillas

Step-by-Step Directions to Cook It:

1. Preheat the air fryer to 380^0F.
2. Sprinkle lime juice over the pork and mix well, set aside. Microwave the pork tortilla and place a damp paper over them for 10 seconds. Add pork and cheese to each tortilla and roll tightly.

Arrange onto a greased foil-lined pan (ensure that the pan fits into the air fryer). Spray the tortillas with cooking spray.

3. Transfer into the air fryer and cook for 10 minutes, flipping halfway through.
4. Serve and enjoy!

Nutritional value per serving:

Calories: 312kcal, Fat: 12g, Carb: 23g, Proteins: 27g

Pork with Couscous

This is another creative way of preparing pork. The meal comes together in 45 minutes, serve and enjoy with your family.
Prep time and cooking time: 45 minutes| Serves: 6

Ingredients To Use:

- 2-1/2 lb. pork loin, boneless and trimmed
- 2 tbsp. olive oil
- 2 cups couscous, cooked
- 3/4 cup. chicken stock
- 1 tsp. dried oregano
- 1/2 tbsp. sweet paprika
- 1/4 tsp. dried marjoram
- 2 and 1/4 tsp. dried sage
- 1/4 tsp. dried rosemary
- 1/2 tbsp. garlic powder
- 1 tsp. dried basil
- Salt and black pepper to taste

Step-by-Step Directions to Cook It:

1. In a pan that fits into the air fryer, add all the ingredients, and mix well. Add the pork and toss to coat, leave to marinate for 1 hour.
2. Preheat the air fryer to 370^{0}F.
3. Transfer to your air fryer and cook for 35 minutes.
4. Serve and enjoy!

Nutritional value per serving:

Calories: 310kcal, Fat: 4g, Carb: 37g, Proteins: 34g

Fennel Flavoured Pork Roast

The fennel boosts the flavor of the pork roast. You may prepare this dish for a special occasion.
Prep time and cooking time: 1hour 10 minutes| Serves: 10

Ingredients To Use:

- 5-1/2 lb. pork loin roast
- 1/4 cup olive oil
- 2 tbsp. chopped rosemary
- 1 tsp. ground fennel
- 1 tbsp. fennel seeds
- 3 garlic cloves, minced
- 2 tsp. crushed red pepper
- Salt and black pepper to taste

Step-by-Step Directions to Cook It:

1. Preheat the air fryer to 350^{0}F.
2. In a food processor, add all the ingredients except the pork. Pulse until you get a paste-like texture. Season the pork with salt and pepper and rub with the paste.
3. Transfer to your air fryer and cook for 30 minutes; reduce the temperature to 300^{0}F. Cook for another 15 minutes.
4. Slice the pork and divide among the plates, enjoy!

Nutritional value per serving:

Calories: 300kcal, Fat: 14g, Carb: 26g, Proteins: 22g

Stuffed Pork Steak

There is nothing as tasty as juicy and tender pork. The stuffing creates unique and delicious pork infused with flavors.
Prep time and cooking time: 30 minutes|

Serves: 4

Ingredients To Use:

- 4 pork loin steak
- 2 tbsp. mustard
- Zest from 2 limes, grated
- Juice from 1 orange
- 2 pickles, chopped
- 6 Swiss cheese, sliced
- Juice from 2 limes
- Zest from 1 orange, grated
- 1 cup. chopped cilantro
- 1 tsp.. dried oregano
- 1 cup. chopped mint
- 4 ham slices
- 2 tbsp. mustard
- 3/4 cup. olive oil
- 2 tsp. ground cumin
- Salt and black pepper to taste

Step-by-Step Directions to Cook It:

1. In a food processor, add lime zest, orange zest, lime juice, orange juice, garlic, oregano, cumin, mint, cilantro, and pulse well.
2. Preheat the air fryer to 340^{0}F, season the steak with salt and pepper. Transfer to a bowl and pour your marinade. Toss to coat and transfer to a working surface.
3. Divide the pickle, cheese, ham, mustard on the pork, roll, and secure with toothpicks. Transfer to the air fryer and cook for 20 minutes.
4. Serve and enjoy with a plate of salad.

Nutritional value per serving:

Calories: 270kcal, Fat: 7g, Carb: 13g, Proteins: 20g

Pork Chops and Roasted Pepper

This piece of a heavenly meal is best enjoyed with cheesy polenta and a glass of good wine.

Prep time and cooking time: 26 minutes| Serves:4

Ingredients To Use:

- 4 pork chops
- 3 tbsp. olive oil
- 2 tbsp. smoked paprika
- 2 roasted bell peppers, chopped
- 3 tbsp. lemon juice
- 2 tbsp. thyme, chopped
- 3 garlic cloves, minced
- Salt and black pepper to taste

Step-by-Step Directions to Cook It:

1. Preheat the air fryer to 400^{0}F.
2. In a bowl that fits into the air fryer, add all the ingredients with the pork chops. Mix thoroughly and transfer into the air fryer. Cook for 16 minutes.
3. Serve and enjoy!

Nutritional value per serving:

Calories: 321kcal, Fat: 6g, Carb: 14g, Proteins: 17g

Pork and Sage Sauce

Feel free to indulge yourself in this irresistible creamy delight. The meat is juicy and tenderwhen combined with the creamy sauce, simply awesome!

Prep time and cooking time: 25 minutes| Serves: 2

Ingredients To Use:

- 2 pork chops
- 2 tbsp. butter
- 1 tbsp. chopped Sage
- 2 garlic cloves, minced
- 1 tbsp. olive oil
- 1 tsp. lemon juice
- 1/2 cup. milk
- 1 shallot, sliced
- Salt and black pepper to taste

Step-by-Step Directions to Cook It:

1. Preheat the air fryer to 370^{0}F.
2. Season the pork chops with salt, pepper, and rub with olive oil. Transfer to the air fryer and cook for 10 minutes, flipping halfway.
3. Meanwhile, heat butter in a pan over medium heat, add garlic, shallot and cook for 2 minutes. Add sage, milk, lemon juice, and cook for 2 minutes. Remove from heat.
4. Serve pork chops with sage sauce, enjoy!

Nutritional value per serving:

Calories: 265kcal, Fat: 6g, Carb: 19g, Proteins: 12g

Bacon-Wrapped Pork Tenderloin

The bacon-wrapped pork tenderloin is soft, juicy, and tender. The addition of the bacon boosts the pork's flavor.

Prep time and cooking time: 25 minutes| Serves: 4

Ingredients To Use:

- 1 lb. pork tenderloin
- 4 bacon strips
- 1/2 tsp. black pepper
- 2 tbsp. Dijon mustard
- 1 tsp. oregano
- 1/2 tsp. garlic powder

Step-by-Step Directions to Cook It:

1. Preheat the air fryer to 360^{0}F.
2. In a bowl, mix mustard with pepper, oregano, and garlic. Coat the tenderloins in the mustard mixture and wrap with the bacon.
3. Transfer to the air fryer basket and cook for 15 minutes, flipping after 7 minutes
4. Serve with sauce of choice and enjoy!

Nutritional value per serving:

Calories: 319kcal, Fat: 21g, Carb: 3g, Proteins: 28g

Marinated Pork Chops and onions

The recipe simply creates a juicy, and tender meat that you won't be able to resist. Enjoy with salad.

Prep time and cooking time: 50 minutes| Serves: 6

Ingredients To Use:

- 2 pork chops
- 2 tsp. mustard
- 1/2 cup. olive oil
- 2 yellow onions, sliced
- 1 tsp. sweet paprika
- 2 garlic cloves, minced
- 1/2 tsp. thyme, dried
- 1/2 tsp. dried oregano
- Salt and black pepper to taste
- Pinch of cayenne pepper

Step-by-Step Directions to Cook It:

1. In a bowl, add all the ingredients and mix well; add the meat and toss to coat. Leave to marinate in the refrigerator for 1 day.
2. Preheat the air fryer to 360^{0}F, pour the meat and onion in a pan that fits into the air fryer, set time to 25 minutes.
3. Serve and enjoy!

Nutritional value per serving:

Calories: 384kcal, Fat: 4g, Carb: 17g, Proteins: 25g

Indian Pork

Spicy and flavorful are the best two words to describe this dish. Enjoy with steamed rice at the side.

Prep time and cooking time: 45 minutes|
Serves: 4

Ingredients To Use:

- 14 oz. pork chops, cut into cubes
- 1 tsp. ginger powder
- 3 tbsp. soy sauce
- 7 oz. coconut milk
- 2 tsp. chili paste
- 1 shallot, chopped
- 1 tsp. ground coriander
- 3 oz. ground peanuts
- 2 tbsp. olive oil
- 2 garlic cloves, minced
- Salt and black pepper to taste

Step-by-Step Directions to Cook It:

1. In a bowl, mix ginger with 1 tsp. chili paste, add half of the following ingredients: soy sauce, oil, garlic. Whisk thoroughly and add the meat, toss to coat. Set aside for 10 minutes.
2. Preheat the air fryer to 400^0F.
3. Transfer the meat into the air fryer basket and cook for 12 minutes, turning halfway.
4. Meanwhile, place a pan over medium heat, add oil and heat until shimmering. Add the rest of the ingredients and cook for 5 minutes.
5. Serve the pork with the coconut mix.

Nutritional value per serving:

Calories: 323kcal, Fat: 11g, Carb: 32g, Proteins: 18g

Pork Burger Cutlets

Pork burger is a tasty and delightful meal.
Prep time and cooking time: 25 minutes |
Serves: 6

Ingredients To Use:

- 1/4 tsp. of dried mango powder
- 1/2 lb. of pork
- 1 tsp. of lemon juice
- 1/2 cup of breadcrumbs
- 1 tbsp. Of fresh coriander leaves.
- Salt
- 1/4 tsp. of chopped ginger
- 1/4 tsp. of red chili powder
- 1/4 tsp. of cumin powder
- 1 chopped green chili
- 1/2 cup of cooked peas

Step-by-Step Directions to Cook It:

1. Mix green chilies, masala, coriander leaves, onions, ginger in a bowl. Add peas, lemon juice, breadcrumbs, and ginger.
2. Make round cutlets from the mixture. Roll the cutlets out.
3. Transfer cutlets to the air fryer and cook for 12 minutes at 150^0F.
4. Serve immediately with ketchup.

Nutritional value per serving:

Calories: 350kcal, Fat: 13g, Carb: 5g, Proteins: 27g

Barbecue Pork Sandwich

Barbecue pork is made by air frying pork at a particular temperature. Follow the instructions verbatim for a truly tasty meal.
Prep time and cooking time: 20 minutes|
Serves: 3

Ingredients To Use:

- 1/2 tsp. of olive oil
- 1/2 cup of water
- 2 white bread slices
- 1/2 flake of crushed garlic
- Pepper and salt
- 1 tbsp. of softened butter
- 1/4 tbsp. of red chili sauce
- 1/4 cup of chopped onion

- 1/2 lb. of cubed pork
- 1/4 tsp. of mustard powder
- 1 capsicum
- 1/2 tbsp. of sugar
- 1/4 tbsp. of Worcestershire sauce
- 1 tbsp. of tomato ketchup

Step-by-Step Directions to Cook It:

1. Remove the edges of the bread slices. Cut it horizontally.
2. In a pan, cook olive oil, Worcestershire sauce, crushed garlic, and sugar. Add tomato ketchup, onion, mustard powder, red chili sauce, salt, and pepper. Stir well until it thickens.
3. Remove the skin of the capsicum and roast well. Slice the capsicum. Mix the capsicum with the ingredients. Add the cubed pork to it. Put the mixture inside the slices of bread.
4. Transfer the sandwich to the air fryer basket. Cook for 15 minutes at 250^{0}F. Flip while cooking for uniformity.

Nutritional value per serving:

Calories: 311kcal, Fat: 10g, Carb: 42g, Proteins: 18g

Japanese Fried Pork Chop

The Japanese have a special way of making pork chop and this recipe has been modified to accommodate the particularities of Japanese cooking with air frying.
Prep time and cooking time: 35 minutes| Serves: 2

Ingredients To Use:

- 1 tbsp. of oil
- 1 tsp. of black pepper
- 2 packets of pounded pork loin
- 1 tsp. of salt
- 1 egg
- Bread crumbs Flour

Step-by-Step Directions to Cook It:

1. Sprinkle pepper and salt on the pork. Allow to rest for about 30 minutes.
2. Whisk egg in a bowl.
3. Put flour and bread crumbs in separate bowls.
4. Put the pork in the egg mixture and transfer to the flour and then bread crumbs.
5. Put coated pork in the air fryer and cook at 390^{0}F for 15 minutes.

Nutritional value per serving:

Calories: 430kcal, Fat: 24g, Carb: 20g, Proteins: 35g

Cheesy Bacon Potato Stuffed

This meal is particularly made during the Thanksgiving and special occasions.
Prep time and cooking time: 55 minutes| Serves: 4

Ingredients To Use:

- 4 medium sized potatoes
- 4 ounces of grated cheese
- 1 chopped small onion
- 2 tbsp. of olive oil
- 2 bacon rashers

Step-by-Step Directions to Cook It:

1. Rub oil on the potatoes. Place it in the air fryer, cook at 356^{0}F for about 10 minutes. Cook till potato is baked.
2. Place bacon and onion in a skillet and fry over medium heat. Add cheese and stir.
3. Mix the potatoes and fried bacon in the air fryer, add cheese and cook for 6 minutes at 356^{0}F.

Nutritional value per serving:

Calories: 198kcal, Fat: 4g, Carb: 36g, Proteins: 7g

Italian Pork

The prosciutto added to the pork adds a delightful taste to this meal.
Prep time and cooking time: 50 minutes|
Serves: 5

Ingredients To Use:

- 2 tbsp. of fresh sage, chopped
- 2 tbsp. of sun-dried tomatoes, chopped
- 2 tbsp. of olive oil
- 1/2 tsp. of black pepper, ground
- 1/4 cup of chopped onion
- 1/4 cup of chopped prosciutto
- 1/2 cup of heavy cream
- 2 tbsp. of fresh parsley, chopped
- 1-1/2 pound of pork tenderloin
- 1/4 tsp. of salt
- 1/2 cup of chicken broth

Step-by-Step Directions to Cook It:

1. Mix tomatoes, pepper, onion, parsley, sage, and prosciutto in a bowl. Add salt and pork tenderloin. Mix the pork and mixture well.
2. Top with cheese. Grease the air fryer with olive oil, place the pork tenderloin on it. Cook for 20 minutes at 350°F.
3. Serve immediately.

Nutritional value per serving:

Calories: 357kcal, Fat: 26g, Carb: 5g, Proteins: 30g

Honey Pork Tenderloin

Honey is naturally sweet and adds a unique flavor to meals. In this recipe, the honey transforms the air fried pork's taste and gives it an unforgettable flavor.
Prep time and cooking time: 1 hour 20 minutes| Serves: 6

Ingredients To Use:

- 1 tbsp. of brown sugar
- 1/3 cup of honey
- 2 tbsp. of balsamic vinegar
- 1 tbsp. of mustard
- 2 pounds of pork tenderloin
- 2 tbsp. of sesame oil.
- 2 tbsp. of soy sauce

Step-by-Step Directions to Cook It:

1. In a bowl, brown sugar, honey, balsamic vinegar, mustard, sesame oil, and soy sauce.
2. Place the pork tenderloin on the air fryer and cook for about 5 minutes. Add the honey mix and cook for 55 minutes.
3. Serve immediately.

Nutritional value per serving:

Calories: 211kcal, Fat: 8g, Carb: 20g, Proteins: 19g

Capers and Pork Chop

The combination of capers and pork chops results in a dashing meal.
Prep time and cooking time: 40 minutes|
Serves: 4

Ingredients To Use:

- 4 of 8 ounces of pork chop
- 3 tbsp. of capers
- 1 sliced lemon
- 3 tbsp. of melted butter
- 4 chopped green onions
- 4 cloves of garlic
- Black pepper and salt

Step-by-Step Directions to Cook It:

1. Rub butter on the pork chop. Spray with pepper and salt. Transfer it to the baking

dish in the air fryer.

2. Add slices of lemon, capers, onion, and garlic. Toss well to coat. Place the mixture in the air fryer.
3. Cook for 30 minutes at 370°F.
4. Serve immediately.

Nutritional value per serving:

Calories: 200kcal, Fat: 9g, Carb: 1g, Proteins: 25g

Pork Chop and asparagus

Asparagus helps neutralize the pork's fatty content and contributes some beneficial nutrients to the body.
Prep time and cooking time: 40 minutes|
Serves: 4

Ingredients To Use:

- 8 ounces of pork chop
- Black pepper and salt
- 1 tsp. of ground cumin
- 8 spears of asparagus
- 1 tbsp. of chopped rosemary

Step-by-Step Directions to Cook It:

1. Sprinkle pork chop with pepper and salt. Add cumin and rosemary. Transfer the mixture to the air fryer basket.
2. Place the asparagus spears on it. Cook for 30 minutes at 360°F.
3. Serve immediately.

Nutritional value per serving:

Calories: 378kcal, Fat: 16g, Carb: 40g, Proteins: 24g

Chapter 7: Meatless Cuisines

Potato Club Sandwich

With this flavor-packed air fryer recipe, making a sandwich with the right proportion of ingredients is possible.
Prep time and cooking time: 30 minutes|
Serves: 3

Ingredients To Use:

- 1 cup of boiled potato
- 6 white bread slices
- 1 medium of small capsicum
- 1 tbsp. of soft butter
- 1/4 cup of chopped onion
- 1/4 tbsp. of Worcestershire sauce
- 1/2 flake of crushed garlic
- 1/4 tbsp. of red chili sauce
- 1/2 tsp. of olive oil

Step-by-Step Directions to Cook It:

1. Cut the edges of the slices of bread.
2. In a bowl, mix olive oil, garlic, onion, chili sauce, and Worcestershire sauce. Remove the capsicum skin and roast. Put the ingredients on the bread slices.
3. Place the sandwich in the air fryer basket. Cook for about 15 minutes at 250^0F.
4. Serve immediately with mint chutney.

Nutritional value per serving:

Calories: 510kcal, Fat: 10g, Carb: 84g, Proteins: 26g

Vegetable Pie

Vegetables always add amazing nutritional benefits to meals. In this recipe, the roasted vegetables do the job exceptionally.
Prep time and cooking time: 30 minutes|

Serves: 3

Ingredients To Use:

- 4 tsp. of powdered sugar
- 1 cup of plain flour
- 2 cups of cold milk
- 1 tbsp. of unsalted butter
- 2 tbsp. of sugar
- 1/2 cup of roasted nuts
- 2 tsp. of lemon juice
- 2 cups of roasted vegetable
- 1/2 tsp. of cinnamon
- 2 tbsp. of sugar

Step-by-Step Directions to Cook It:

1. Mix butter, sugar, and flour in a bowl. Add cold milk, mix till it forms a dough. Allow resting for 10 minutes.
2. Cut a circle out of the dough. Put the dough in a pie tin.
3. In a pan, mix roasted nuts, roasted vegetables, sugar, cinnamon, and lemon juice. Cook over low flame. Pour the mixture inside the pie tin.
4. Transfer the pie tin to the air fryer basket. Cook till it is brown.
5. Allow the pan to cool and serve with cream.

Nutritional value per serving:

Calories: 195kcal, Fat: 6g, Carb: 33g, Proteins: 5g

Cottage Cheese Kebab

The lemon juice used in this recipe adds a unique flavor to this cheese kebab recipe.
Prep time and cooking time: 35 minutes|
Serves: 5

Ingredients To Use:

- 1-1/2 tsp. of salt
- 5 chopped green chilies
- 3 tsp. of lemon juice
- 3 eggs
- 2 tbsp. of coriander powder
- 2 cups of cubed cottage cheese
- 1-1/2 tbsp. of ginger paste
- 3 tbsp. of chopped capsicum
- 1-1/2 tsp. of garlic paste
- 2 tbsp. of peanut flour
- 3 tsp. of lemon juice

Step-by-Step Directions to Cook It:

1. Put the cubed cheese in the cornflour and coat. Add onion, green chilies, ginger paste, garlic paste, salt, lemon juice, coriander powder, and capsicum.
2. Break egg inside another bowl, add salt, and whisk.
3. Put the cubed cheese in the egg mixture. Spray with sesame seeds. Put in the fridge for about an hour.
4. Put the cheese kebab in the air fryer basket. Cook at 290^{0}F for 25 minutes. Flip while cooking to give uniformity.

Nutritional value per serving:

Calories: 30kcal, Fat: 0.3g, Carb: 1.5g, Proteins: 4g

Cottage Cheese Fingers

Cheese fingers can be made by frying or baking. The air fryer makes the cooked cheese fingers crispy.
Prep time and cooking time: 25 minutes|
Serves: 4

Ingredients To Use:

- 2 cups of dry breadcrumbs
- 2 tsp. of red chili flakes
- 2 cups of cottage cheese fingers
- 2 tsp. of oregano

- 1 tsp. of pepper powder
- 1-1/2 tbsp. of ginger-garlic paste
- 1 tsp. of pepper powder
- 4 eggs
- 1 tsp. of red chili powder
- 2 tsp. of salt
- 6 tbsp. of cornflour

Step-by-Step Directions to Cook It:

1. In a bowl, mix ginger-garlic paste, lemon juice, salt, pepper powder, red chili powder, cornflour, and eggs.
2. In another bowl, mix red chili flakes, breadcrumbs, and oregano. Mix the 2 mixtures. Add cottage cheese fingers. Cover the mixture and leave for a while.
3. Place the cheese fingers inside the air fryer basket. Cook for about 15 minutes at 160^{0}F.

Nutritional value per serving:

Calories: 85kcal, Fat: 3g, Carb: 5g, Proteins: 12g

Onion Galette

Onion is rich in vitamins, and it reduces the risk of having cancer. It also helps to moderate blood pressure. And all these benefits explain why an onion galette is a healthy meal.
Prep time and cooking time: 35 minutes|
Serves: 3

Ingredients To Use:

- 2 tbsp. of coriander leaves, fresh
- 2 medium sized onion
- Pepper and salt
- 3 tsp. of chopped ginger
- 3 chopped green chilies
- 1-1/2 cup of crushed peanuts
- 1-1/2 tbsp. of lemon juice
- 2 tbsp. of garam masala

Step-by-Step Directions to Cook It:

1. In a bowl, mix garam masala, onion, chopped ginger, coriander leaves, green chilies, salt, pepper, and lemon juice. Mix well till it forms a flat and round galette.
2. Sprinkle water on the galettes. Place the galettes in the crushed peanuts.
3. Transfer the galettes to the air fryer basket. Cook for about 25 minutes at 160^{0}F.
4. Serve immediately with ketchup.

Nutritional value per serving:

Calories: 310kcal, Fat: 14g, Carb: 43g, Proteins: 13g

Cauliflower Galette

Try out this recipe for a truly delectable meal.
Prep time and cooking time: 35 minutes|
Serves: 3

Ingredients To Use:

- 2 tbsp. of coriander leaves, fresh
- Pepper and salt
- 3 tsp .of chopped ginger
- 1-1/2 tbsp. of lemon juice
- 2 cups of cauliflower
- 1-1/2 cup of crushed peanuts
- 2 tbsp. of garam masala
- 3 chopped green chilies

Step-by-Step Directions to Cook It:

1. In a bowl, mix garam masala, cauliflower, ginger, coriander leaves, green chilies, lemon juice, pepper, and salt. Mix till it forms flat and round galettes.
2. Spray the galette with water. Place the galette inside the crushed peanuts.
3. Transfer the galettes into the air fryer basket. Cook at 160^{0}F for 25 minutes. Flip while cooking.
4. Serve immediately with ketchup.

Nutritional value per serving:

Calories: 300kcal, Fat: 20g, Carb: 30g,

Proteins: 10g

Cabbage Fritters

Cabbage fritters are a high-calorie meal, but the cabbage reduces the unhealthy calories.
Prep time and cooking time: 30 minutes|
Serves: 4

Ingredients To Use:

- 2 chopped green chilies
- 2 cups of cabbage
- Pepper and salt
- 3 tsp. of chopped ginger
- 2 tbsp. of garam masala
- 1-1/2 tbsp. of lemon juice
- 1-1/2 cup of crushed peanuts
- 2 tbsp. of coriander leaves, fresh

Step-by-Step Directions to Cook It:

1. In a bowl, mix garam masala, cabbage, ginger, coriander leaves, green chilies, lemon juice, pepper, and salt. Mix until it forms 4 flat and round fritters.
2. Sprinkle water on the fritters. Place the fritters inside the crushed peanuts and coat.
3. Transfer the fritters inside the air fryer basket. Cook at 160^{0}F for 20-25 minutes. Flip while cooking.
4. Serve immediately with chutney.

Nutritional value per serving:

Calories: 360kcal, Fat: 23g, Carb: 25g, Proteins: g

Cottage Cheese Galettes

Cottage cheese galettes is a creamy meal that provides vitamins to the body.
Prep time and cooking time: 35 minutes|
Serves: 3

Ingredients To Use:

- 1-1/2 cup of crushed peanuts

- Pepper and salt
- 3 tsp. of chopped ginger
- 2 tbsp. of garam masala
- 2 tbsp. of coriander leaves, fresh
- 1-1/2 tbsp. of lemon juice
- 2 cups of grated cottage cheese
- 3 chopped green chilies

Step-by-Step Directions to Cook It:

1. In a bowl, mix all the ingredients except crushed peanuts. Mix till it forms flat and round galettes.
2. Sprinkle water on the galettes. Place the galettes in the crushed peanuts.
3. Transfer the galettes to the air fryer basket. Cook at 160^{0}F for 25 minutes.
4. Serve immediately with ketchup.

Nutritional value per serving:

Calories: 131kcal, Fat: 7g, Carb: 9g, Proteins: 10g

Gourd Galette

With your air fryer, you can prepare a rare delicacy such as gourd galette.
Prep time and cooking time: 30 minutes|
Serves: 4

Ingredients To Use:

- 1-1/2 cup of crushed peanuts
- Pepper and salt
- 3 tsp. of chopped ginger
- 2 tbsp. of garam masala
- 2 tbsp. of coriander leaves, fresh
- 1-1/2 tbsp. of lemon juice
- 2 cups of the sliced gourd
- 3 chopped green chilies

Step-by-Step Directions to Cook It:

1. In a bowl, mix garam masala, slices of gourd, ginger, coriander leaves, green chilies, lemon juice, pepper, and salt.

Make 3 flat and round galettes out of it.
2. Spray the galette with water. Place the galette inside the crushed peanuts.
3. Transfer the galettes into the air fryer basket. Cook at 160^{0}F for 25 minutes. Flip while cooking.
4. Serve immediately with ketchup.

Nutritional value per serving:

Calories: 344kcal, Fat: 23g, Carb: 29g, Proteins: 15g

Cottage Cheese Patties

Using an air fryer to create these patties makes the meal soft and palatable.
Prep time and cooking time: 25 minutes|
Serves: 2

Ingredients To Use:

- Pepper and salt
- 1/4 tsp. of red chili powder
- 1/4 tsp. of chopped ginger
- 1 tbsp. of coriander leaves, fresh
- 1 tbsp. of lemon juice
- 1/4 tsp. of cumin powder
- 1 cups of grated cottage cheese
- 1 chopped green chilies

Step-by-Step Directions to Cook It:

1. In a bowl, mix cottage cheese, ginger, green chili, lemon juice, coriander leaves, red chili powder, cumin powder. Make patties out of the mixture.
2. Place the patties in the air fryer basket. Cook for 10 minutes at 150^{0}F. Flip while cooking.
3. Serve immediately with chutney.

Nutritional value per serving:

Calories: kcal, Fat: g, Carb: g, Proteins: g

Garlic and Cheese French Fries

Everyone loves French fries but may avoid it due to the high-calorie. Well, you do not need to avoid this recipe because the starch is well balanced to provide a healthy meal. Prep time and cooking time: 30 minutes| Serves: 4

Ingredients To Use:

- 1 cup of molten cheese
- 1 tbsp. of olive oil
- 1 tbsp. of lemon juice
- 2 medium sized potatoes
- 1 tsp. of mixed herbs
- 1/2 tsp. of red chili flakes
- 2 tsp. of garlic powder
- salt

Step-by-Step Directions to Cook It:

1. boil and bleach the potatoes. Cut it into pieces.
2. In a pan, mix olive oil, mixed herbs, red chili flakes, salt, molten cheese, garlic powder, and lemon juice. Cook over medium heat till it thickens.
3. Put the potatoes in the marinade. Place the coated fries in the air fryer basket. Cook for 25 minutes at 200⁰F.
4. Serve immediately.

Nutritional value per serving:

Calories: 690kcal, Fat: 50g, Carb: 50g, Proteins: 10g

Pineapple Kebab

All the ingredients in this recipe can be purchased at the local grocery store, therefore fulfilling this book's major promises to provide healthy, accessible meals.
Prep time and cooking time: 35 minutes| Serves: 4

Ingredients To Use:

- 1-1/2 tsp. of salt
- 2 cups of pineapple cubes
- 3 tbsp. of cream
- 3 tsp. of lemon juice
- 3 eggs
- 5 chopped green chilies
- 1-1/2 tsp. of salt
- 3 tbsp. of chopped capsicum
- 3 medium chopped onion
- 2-1/2 tbsp. of white sesame seeds
- 1-1/2 tbsp. of ginger paste
- 2 tsp. of garam masala
- 1-1/2 tsp. of garlic paste

Step-by-Step Directions to Cook It:

1. In a food processor, blend all the ingredients except eggs and pineapple.
2. Put the pineapple in the mixture and coat.
3. Break the eggs in a bowl, sprinkle salt to taste. Put the coated pineapple inside the egg mixture. Put the coated pineapple on a stick.
4. Place it in the air fryer basket. Cook at 160⁰F for 25 minutes. Flip while cooking.
5. Serve immediately.

Nutritional value per serving:

Calories: 177kcal, Fat: 6g, Carb: 30g, Proteins: 10g

Banana Croquette

Banana is highly recommended for weight loss, and its addition to this croquette recipe makes it a great meal for vegetarians.
Prep time and cooking time: 35 minutes| Serves: 3

Ingredients To Use:

- 1-1/2 tsp. of salt
- 2 cups of banana slices
- 3 tbsp. of cream
- 3 tsp. of lemon juice

- 3 eggs
- 5 chopped green chilies
- 1-1/2 tsp. of salt
- 3 tbsp. of chopped capsicum
- 3 medium of chopped onion
- 2-1/2 tbsp. of white sesame seeds
- 1-1/2 tbsp. of ginger paste
- 2 tsp. of garam masala
- 1-1/2 tsp. of garlic paste

Step-by-Step Directions to Cook It:

1. In a blender, grind the ingredients except for banana and eggs. Blend till it forms a paste. Put the banana slices inside the paste.
2. Whisk the egg in a bowl, place the coated banana inside the egg mixture. Then back to the paste. Put the coated banana slice on a stick.
3. Transfer it to the air fryer basket. Cook for about 20-25 minutes at 160^0F. Flip over while cooking.
4. Serve immediately.

Nutritional value per serving:

Calories: 90kcal, Fat: 0.5g, Carb: 23g, Proteins: 2g

Apricot Kebab

Apricot is an amazing fruit and adds an incredible flavor to this kebab recipe.
Prep time and cooking time: 25 minutes|
Serves: 2

Ingredients To Use:

- 3 eggs
- 2 cups of fresh apricots
- 3 medium chopped onions
- 3 tsp. of lemon juice
- 5 chopped green chilies
- 2 tsp. of garam masala
- 2-1/2 tbsp. of white sesame seeds
- 1-1/2 tbsp. of ginger paste

- 1-1/2 tsp. of garlic paste
- 1-1/2 tsp. of salt

Step-by-Step Directions to Cook It:

1. Blend onion, green chilies, ginger paste, garlic paste, salt, lemon juice, and garam masala in a blender. Blend till it forms a paste.
2. Whisk eggs in a bowl and put the apricot in it.
3. Put the apricot in the paste and coat. Then inside the sesame seed and coat again
4. Put the apricot on a stick. Transfer it to the air fryer basket. Cook at 160^0F for 25 minutes.
5. Serve immediately.

Nutritional value per serving:

Calories: 141kcal, Fat: 2g, Carb: 15g, Proteins: 23g

Cauliflower Kebab

Cauliflower kebab is another super flavorful meal. Lemon juice is used to give the meal an exceptional and great feel.
Prep time and cooking time: 30 minutes |
Serves: 5

Ingredients To Use:

- 2 cups of cauliflower florets
- 1-1/2 tsp. of salt
- 3 medium chopped onions
- 2-1/2 tbsp. of white sesame seeds
- 3 tsp. of lemon juice
- 5 green chopped chilies
- 2 tsp. of garam masala
- 3 eggs
- 1-1/2 tbsp. of ginger paste
- 1-1/2 tsp. of garlic paste

Step-by-Step Directions to Cook It:

1. In a blender, grind the ingredients except for cauliflower florets and eggs.

Blend till it forms a paste. Put the floret inside the paste.

2. Whisk the egg in a bowl, place the coated floret inside the egg mixture. Then back to the paste. Put the coated floret slice on a stick.

3. Transfer the floret stick to the air fryer basket. Cook for about 20-25 minutes at 160^0F. Flip over while cooking.

4. Serve immediately.

Nutritional value per serving:

Calories: 82kcal, Fat:6 g, Carb: 10g, Proteins: 5g

Broccoli Tikka

Though broccoli may not be the tastiest of all vegetables, it adds an incredible flavor to this meal.

Prep time and cooking time: 35 minutes| Serves: 3

Ingredients To Use:

- 2 cups of broccoli florets
- 1-1/2 tsp. of garlic paste
- 3 medium chopped onions
- 3 tsp. of lemon juice
- 5 green chopped chilies
- 1-1/2 tsp. of salt
- 2 tsp. of garam masala
- 1-1/2 tbsp. of ginger paste
- 2-1/2 tbsp. of white sesame seeds
- 3 eggs

Step-by-Step Directions to Cook It:

1. In a food processor, grind the ingredients except for cauliflower florets and eggs. Blend till it forms a paste. Put the broccoli inside the paste.

2. Whisk the eggs in a bowl, place the coated broccoli inside the egg mixture. Then back to the sesame seeds and coat well. Put the coated broccoli on a stick.

3. Transfer the broccoli stick to the air fryer basket. Cook for about 20-25 minutes at 160^0F. Flip over while cooking.

4. Serve immediately.

Nutritional value per serving:

Calories: 420kcal, Fat: 31g, Carb: 10g, Proteins: 27g

Cottage Cheese Gnocchis

Cheese gnocchi is a meal with a sweet and amazing taste.

Prep time and cooking time: | Serves:

Ingredients To Use:

- 2 tsp. of vinegar
- 1-1/2 cup of all-purpose flour
- 2 tbsp. of oil
- 1/2 tsp. of salt
- 2 tsp. of ginger-garlic paste
- 5 tbsp. of water
- 2 tsp. of soya sauce
- 2 cups of grated cottage cheese

Step-by-Step Directions to Cook It:

1. In a bowl, mix flour, water, and salt to form a dough. Knead well.

2. In a pan, cook cottage cheese, oil, ginger-garlic paste, soya sauce, and vinegar. Cook till it thickens.

3. Put the filling mixture on each dough and wrap. Put the gnocchi in the air fryer basket. Cook for 20 minutes at 200^0F.

4. Serve immediately with ketchup.

Nutritional value per serving:

Calories: 7kcal, Fat: 0.04g, Carb: 0.5g, Proteins: 0.1g

Bottle Gourd Flat Cakes

With the use of bottle gourds in this recipe, the taste is totally unique, with an outburst of flavors on the tastebuds.

Prep time and cooking time: 30 minutes|
Serves: 4

Ingredients To Use:

- 2 tbsp. of garam masala
- 3 chopped green chilies
- 2 cups of bottle gourd slices
- 1-1/2 tbsp. of lemon juice
- 3 tsp. of chopped ginger
- Pepper and salt
- 2 tbsp. of fresh coriander leaves

Step-by-Step Directions to Cook It:

1. Mix all the ingredients in a bowl, add water until it forms a paste. Put the bottle gourd in it and coat well.
2. Transfer the coated bottle gourd to the air fryer basket. Cook for 25 minutes at 160°F.
3. Serve immediately with ketchup.

Nutritional value per serving:

Calories: 16kcal, Fat: 0.1g, Carb: 4g, Proteins: 1g

Snake Gourd Cakes

Snake gourd cake is a great and healthy cake. Try this recipe and enjoy the wonderful taste. Prep time and cooking time: 30 minutes| Serves: 4

Ingredients To Use:

- 2 tbsp. of garam masala
- 3 chopped green chilies
- 2 cups of sliced snake gourd
- 1-1/2 tbsp. of lemon juice
- 3 tsp. of chopped ginger
- Pepper and salt
- 2 tbsp. of fresh coriander leaves

Step-by-Step Directions to Cook It:

1. In a bowl, mix all the ingredients, add water till it forms a paste. Put the slices of snack gourd in it and coat.

2. Transfer the slices of snack gourd to the air fryer basket. Bake for 25 minutes at 160°F.
3. Serve immediately.

Nutritional value per serving:

Calories: 89kcal, Fat: 5g, Carb: 8g, Proteins: 6g

Cabbage Flat Cakes

Cabbage is a low-calorie fruit vegetable, and on its addition to the regular ingredients of a pound cake, it transforms the snack into a delicious and healthy combination. It is best made during a special gathering or occasion. Prep time and cooking time: 35 minutes| Serves: 4

Ingredients To Use:

- 3 tsp. of ginger finely chopped
- 2 tbsp. of garam masala
- 3 chopped green chilies
- 2 cups of halved cabbage leaves
- 1-1/2 tbsp. of lemon juice
- 2 tbsp. of fresh coriander leaves
- Pepper and salt

Step-by-Step Directions to Cook It:

1. Mix all the ingredients in a bowl, add water until it forms a paste. Avoid adding too much water. Put the cabbage in it and coat well.
2. Transfer the coated cabbage to the air fryer basket. Bake for 25 minutes at 160°F.
3. Serve immediately with ketchup.

Nutritional value per serving:

Calories: 22kcal, Fat: 0.5g, Carb: 6g, Proteins: 2g

Bitter Gourd Cakes

Bitter gourd, also known as bitter melon, has

many nutritional benefits. Bitter gourd helps to reduce and maintain sugar level in the blood.

Prep time and cooking time: 35 minutes| Serves: 4

Ingredients To Use:

- 1-/2 tbsp. of lemon juice
- 2 tbsp. of garam masala
- 2 tbsp. of fresh coriander leaves
- 2 cups of sliced bitter gourd
- Pepper and salt
- 3 chopped green chilies
- 3 tsp. of ginger finely chopped

Step-by-Step Directions to Cook It:

1. Mix all the ingredients in a bowl, add water until it forms a paste. Avoid adding too much water. Put the bitter gourd in it and coat well.
2. Transfer the coated bitter gourd to the air fryer basket. Bake for 25 minutes at 160^0F.
3. Serve immediately with ketchup.

Nutritional value per serving:

Calories: 21kcal, Fat: 0.1g, Carb: 4g, Proteins: 1g

Pumpkin Galette

Pumpkin is a good source of vitamin A; it also has low calories. Pumpkin galette can be made in different ways. Below is a unique way of making it.

Prep time and cooking time: 30 minutes| Serves: 4

Ingredients To Use:

- 2 tbsp. of garam masala
- 3 chopped green chilies
- 1 cup of sliced pumpkin
- 1-1/2 tbsp. of lemon juice
- 3 tsp. of chopped ginger

- Pepper and salt
- 2 tbsp. of fresh coriander leaves

Step-by-Step Directions to Cook It:

1. In a bowl, mix the ingredients. Make 4 flat and round galettes from it. Sprinkle water on the galettes.
2. Transfer the galettes to the air fryer and cook for 25 minutes at 160^0F.
3. Serve with ketchup.

Nutritional value per serving:

Calories: 350kcal, Fat: 22g, Carb: 29g, Proteins: 15g

Radish Flat Cakes

Radish is mostly served as a salad due to its high fiber content.

Prep time and cooking time: 35 minutes| Serves: 5

Ingredients To Use:

- 2 tbsp. of garam masala
- 3 chopped green chilies
- 2 cups of sliced radish
- 1-1/2 tbsp. of lemon juice
- 3 tsp. of chopped ginger
- Pepper and salt
- 2 tbsp. of fresh coriander leaves

Step-by-Step Directions to Cook It:

1. Mix all the ingredients in a bowl, add water until it forms a paste. Put the radish in it and coat well.
2. Transfer the coated radish to the air fryer basket. Bake for 25 minutes at 160^0F.
3. Serve immediately with ketchup.

Nutritional value per serving:

Calories: 523kcal, Fat: 24g, Carb: 53g, Proteins: 12g

Mushroom Wonton

Mushroom wonton can also be called mushroom pie. It is prepared in almost the same way as a regular pie, but the ingredients are quite different.

Prep time and cooking time: 20 minutes | Serves: 2

Ingredients To Use:

- 1-1/2 cup of all-purpose flour
- 2 tbsp. of oil
- 1/2 tsp. of salt
- 2 tsp. of ginger-garlic paste
- 5 tbsp. of water
- 2 tsp. of soya sauce
- 2 tsp. of vinegar
- 2 cups of cubed mushroom

Step-by-Step Directions to Cook It:

1. In a big bowl, mix the flour, salt, and water. Knead well to form a smooth dough.
2. In a pan, put oil, mushroom, ginger-garlic paste, soya sauce, vinegar, and cook.
3. Place the dough on a working surface. Fill the dough with the mushroom mixture. Use water to seal the edges.
4. Transfer the wonton to your air fryer basket. Set the air fryer to 200^{0}F and cook for 20 minutes.

Nutritional value per serving:

Calories: 71kcal, Fat: 2g, Carb: 13g, Proteins: 3g

Asparagus Galette

Asparagus is also called sparrow grass. Asparagus is fast and easy to cook, and it improves digestive health, and also lowers blood pressure.

Prep time and cooking time: 30 minutes| Serves:

Ingredients To Use:

- 2 cups of minced asparagus
- 1-1/2 tbsp. of lemon juice
- 3 tsp. of chopped ginger
- Pepper and salt
- 2 tbsp. of freshly chopped coriander leaves
- 3 chopped green chilies

Step-by-Step Directions to Cook It:

1. In a bowl, mix all the ingredients. Make flat and round galettes from the mixture. Spray the galettes with water.
2. Transfer it to your air fryer. Set the air fryer to 160^{0}F, cook for 25 minutes.
3. Serve with tomato ketchup.

Nutritional value per serving:

Calories: 378kcal, Fat: 28g, Carb: 24g, Proteins: 10g

Chapter 8: Side Snacks and Appetizers

Fish Nuggets

Fish nuggets are like chicken nuggets, but with fewer calories

Prep time and cooking time: 25 minutes| Serves: 4

Ingredients To Use:

- 1 tbsp. of smoked paprika
- 5 tbsp. of flour
- 28 ounces of skinless fish fillets
- Cooking spray
- 5 tbsp. of water
- 1 tsp. of dried dill
- 3 ounces of panko bread crumbs
- 1 egg
- 4 tbsp. of homemade mayonnaise
- Black pepper and salt
- 1/2 lemon juice
- 1 tbsp. of garlic powder

Step-by-Step Directions to Cook It:

1. Mix water and flour in a bowl. Add pepper, egg, and salt. Whisk.
2. In another bowl, mix paprika, panko, and garlic powder.
3. Put pieces of fish inside the egg mixture and the flour mixture. Transfer it to the air fryer basket. Cook for 10-12 minutes at 400^0F.
4. Mix lemon juice, mayonnaise, and dill in another bowl.
5. Serve fish nugget with lemon juice mixture.

Nutritional value per serving:

Calories: 300kcal, Fat: 11g, Carb: 21g, Proteins: 17g

Chestnut and Shrimp Rolls

Chestnut is an edible nut with low protein and fat content. It also contains vitamin C, which makes it a good addition for a healthy snack.

Prep time and cooking time: 25 minutes| Serves: 4

Ingredients To Use:

- 1 clove of minced garlic
- 1 egg yolk
- 8 ounces of chopped water chestnuts
- 3 chopped scallions
- 2 tbsp. of olive oil
- 2 cups of chopped cabbage
- 1/2 pounds of chopped shiitake mushrooms
- Black pepper and salt
- 1/2 pound of chopped cooked shrimp
- 1 tsp. of grated ginger
- 1 tbsp. of water
- 6 wrappers of spring roll

Step-by-Step Directions to Cook It:

1. Put oil in a pan and heat over medium heat. Add mushrooms, ginger, cabbage, and salt. Add shrimps, garlic, pepper, and scallions. Cook for about 2 minutes
2. Mix water and egg in a bowl. Stir.
3. Place the roll wrappers on a flat surface. Put veggie mix and shrimps on it. Seal it with egg wash. Transfer it to the air fryer basket. Cook for 16 minutes at 360^0F.
4. Serve immediately as an appetizer.

Nutritional value per serving:

Calories: 142kcal, Fat: 5g, Carb: 15g, Proteins: 5g

Seafood Appetizer

This recipe is an explosion of seafood. Crabmeat and shrimp paired together produce an exotic taste.

Prep time and cooking time: 35 minutes| Serves: 4

Ingredients To Use:
- 1 cup of flaked crabmeat
- 1 tbsp. of butter
- 1 cup of chopped green bell pepper
- 2 tbsp. of bread crumbs
- 1/2 cup of chopped yellow onion
- 1 cup of chopped celery
- 1 tsp. of sweet paprika
- 1 tsp. of Worcestershire sauce
- 1 cup of homemade mayonnaise
- Black pepper and salt
- 1 cup of peeled baby shrimp

Step-by-Step Directions to Cook It:
1. Mix bell pepper, mayonnaise, shrimps, pepper, onion, salt, crab meat, and celery in a bowl.
2. Put Worcestershire sauce and stir. Transfer the mixture to a baking sheet that fits the air fryer.
3. Add butter and spray bread crumbs. Cook for 20-25 minutes at 320^0F.
4. Serve immediately as an appetizer, top with paprika.

Nutritional value per serving:

Calories: 201kcal, Fat: 5g, Carb: 10g, Proteins: 5g

Salmon Meatballs

Salmon is rich in fatty acid and protein, and when prepared as meatballs, it's incredible.

Prep time and cooking time: 25 minutes| Serves: 4

Ingredients To Use:

- 1 egg white
- 1/2 tsp. of paprika
- 3 tbsp. of minced cilantro
- Cooking spray
- 1 pound of chopped and skinless salmon
- 1/2 tsp. of ground oregano
- 1 chopped small onion, yellow
- 2 cloves of garlic
- Black pepper and salt
- 1/4 cup of panko

Step-by-Step Directions to Cook It:
1. Get a food processor, mix salt, cilantro, paprika, salmon, salt, and garlic cloves. Add egg white, oregano, panko, and onion. And blend well. Shape into meatball form.
2. Transfer the meatball to the air fryer basket. Sprinkle with cooking spray. Cook for about 10-12 minutes at 320^0F.
3. Serve the meatballs as an appetizer.

Nutritional value per serving:

Calories: 290kcal, Fat: 15g, Carb: 25g, Proteins: 27g

Chicken Wings

Chicken wings are healthy and taste great. What could be better?

Prep time and cooking time: 1 hour 10 minutes| Serves: 2

Ingredients To Use:
- 1/4 cup of honey
- 16 pieces of chicken wings
- 3/4 cup of potato starch
- 4 tbsp. of minced garlic
- 1/4 cup of butter
- Black pepper and salt

Step-by-Step Directions to Cook It:
1. Mix pepper, chicken wings, potato starch, and salt in a bowl. Put the mixture in the air fryer basket.

2. Cook at 360^{0}F for about 25 minutes, increase the temperature to 400^{0}F for 5 minutes.
3. Get another pan, put butter, and heat over medium heat. Put garlic and mix. Cook for about 5 minutes. Add honey, salt, and pepper. Cook for 20 minutes over medium heat.
4. Place chicken wings in bowls and serve with honey sauce as an appetizer.

Nutritional value per serving:

Calories: 90kcal, Fat: 7g, Carb: 0g, Proteins: 14g

Chicken Breast Rolls

Chicken breast roll is mostly eaten as an appetizer. It is taste perfect and is healthy.
Prep time and cooking time: 35 minutes|
Serves: 4

Ingredients To Use:
● 1 cup of chopped dried tomatoes
● 2 cups of baby spinach
● Olive oil
● Black pepper and salt
● 4 skinless and boneless chicken breasts
● 4 slices of mozzarella
● 1-1/2 tbsp. of Italian seasoning

Step-by-Step Directions to Cook It:
1. Use a meat tenderizer to flatten chicken breasts. Put spinach, pepper, mozzarella, Italian seasoning, and salt. Roll it and seal.
2. Transfer it to the air fryer basket. Spray oil on the chicken breast roll. Cook for 18 minutes on both side at 375^{0}F.
3. Serve the chicken breast roll immediately as an appetizer.

Nutritional value per serving:

Calories: 170kcal, Fat: 4g, Carb: 0g, Proteins: 35g

Chicken Breast Sticks Crispy

This crispy chicken recipe will leave you drooling for more. outturn on your air fryer and start cooking.
Prep time and cooking time: 30 minutes|
Serves: 4

Ingredients To Use:
● 1 cup of panko bread crumbs
● 1 grated lemon zest
● 1 pound of boneless and skinless chicken breast
● 3/4 cup of white flour
● Black pepper and salt
● 1 tsp. of sweet paprika
● 1 egg
● 1/2 tbsp. of olive oil

Step-by-Step Directions to Cook It:
1. Mix salt, lemon zest, paprika, pepper, and flour in a bowl.
2. Put the egg in a separate bowl and whisk.
3. Put panko bread crumbs in another bowl. Coat the chicken in flour mixture, egg, and panko. Transfer them to the air fryer basket. Spray oil on them. Cook for 9 minutes on both sides at 400^{0}F.
4. Place them on a platter, serve immediately as an appetizer.

Nutritional value per serving:

Calories: 168kcal, Fat: 4g, Carb: 0g, Proteins: 33g

Beef Rolls

Beef roll is an amazing appetizer with high protein.
Prep time and cooking time: 25 minutes|
Serves: 4

Ingredients To Use:
● 1 cup of baby spinach
● 3 tbsp. of pesto

- 2 pounds of flattened beef steak
- 6 slices of provolone cheese
- Black pepper and salt
- 3 ounces of chopped, roasted red bell pepper.

Step-by-Step Directions to Cook It:

1. Place the flattened beef steak on a flat surface, put pesto over it. Put bell peppers, cheese, pepper, spinach, and salt.
2. Roll the beefsteak, use a toothpick to hold it, sprinkle pepper and salt again.
3. Transfer it to the air fryer basket. Cook for 14 minutes at 400^{0}F.
4. Allow cooling before serving as an appetizer.

Nutritional value per serving:

Calories: 296kcal, Fat: 17g, Carb: 5g, Proteins: 36g

Empanadas

This empanadas recipe combines beef and other flavor-rich ingredients to make a filling.
Prep time and cooking time: 35 minutes|
Serves: 4

Ingredients To Use:
- 1 chopped onion, yellow
- 1 chopped green bell pepper
- 1 empanada shells, package
- 4cup of tomato salsa
- 1 tbsp. of olive oil
- 1/2 tsp. of ground cumin
- Black pepper and salt
- 1 pound of ground beef meat
- 2 cloves of garlic
- 1 egg yolk and 1 tbsp. of water

Step-by-Step Directions to Cook It:

1. Put oil in a pan and heat over medium heat. Add beef, make it brown on every side.

2. Add bell pepper, onion, pepper, tomato salsa, garlic, and salt. Cook for about 14 minutes.
3. Put the meat into empanadas shells. Rub egg wash all over it and seal.
4. Put it in the steam basket in the air fryer. Cook for 10 minutes at 350^{0}F.
5. Serve immediately in a bowl as an appetizer.

Nutritional value per serving:

Calories: 300kcal, Fat: 20g, Carb: 33g, Proteins: 15g

Lamb Meatballs

Lamb is rich in protein, and as meatballs, it can serve as a fantastic appetizer.
Prep time and cooking time: 20 minutes|
Serves: 10

Ingredients To Use:
- 1 slice of toasted, crumbled bread
- 4 ounces of minced lamb meat
- 1/2 tbsp. of grated lemon peels
- Black pepper and salt
- 1 tbsp. of chopped oregano
- 4 ounces of minced lamb meat

Step-by-Step Directions to Cook It:

1. Mix salt, feta, lemon peels, bread crumbs, pepper, and oregano in a bowl. Scoop into 10 meatball shape.
2. Transfer it to the air fryer basket. Cook for 8-10 minutes at 400^{0}F.
3. Serve immediately as an appetizer.

Nutritional value per serving:

Calories: 250kcal, Fat: 15g, Carb: 22g, Proteins: 35g

Beef Party Rolls

When white wine is used to make beef party rolls, it results in an exceptional taste.

Prep time and cooking time: 35 minutes|
Serves: 4

Ingredients To Use:

- 1 tbsp. of melted butter
- 7 ounces of white wine
- Black pepper and salt
- 4 slices of ham
- 4 cutlets of beef
- 14 ounces of beef stock
- 8 sage leaves

Step-by-Step Directions to Cook It:

1. Put beef stock in a pan and heat over medium heat. Put wine and cook. For some minutes.
2. Sprinkle pepper and salt over cutlets. Pour sage on it and roll it in ham slices.
3. Rub butter on rolls. Transfer it to the air fryer basket. Cook for about 15 minutes at 400^{0}F.
4. Serve immediately with gravy.

Nutritional value per serving:

Calories: 296kcal, Fat: 16g, Carb: 2g, Proteins: 36g

Pork Rolls

Pork rolls smell good and taste great. The cumin and chili powder introduces a sharp spicy taste to the rolls
Prep time and cooking time: 50 minutes|
Serves: 4

Ingredients To Use:

- 1 chopped red onion
- 1 tsp. of cinnamon powder
- 2 tbsp. of olive oil
- 15 ounces of pork fillet
- 1 clove of garlic
- 1-1/2 tsp. of ground cumin
- 1/2 tsp. of chili powder
- 2 tbsp. of olive oil

- 3 tbsp. of chopped parsley

Step-by-Step Directions to Cook It:

1. Mix salt, onion, garlic, chili powder, cinnamon powder, and parsley. Add cumin, oil, and pepper. Mix well.
2. Place the pork fillet on a flat surface. Use a meat tenderizer to flatten it.
3. Put the onions on the pork and roll it tight.
4. Transfer the rolled pork to the air fryer basket. Cook at 360^{0}F for 30-35 minutes.
5. Serve immediately as an appetizer.

Nutritional value per serving:

Calories: 290kcal, Fat: 15g, Carb: 0g, Proteins: 30g

Beef Patties

You don't need to queue at a burger shop before you get a great burger. You can air-fry an even healthier, tastier burger by making patties with this recipe.
Prep time and cooking time: 20 minutes|
Serves: 4

Ingredients To Use:

- 1 chopped leek
- 14 ounces of minced beef
- 1/2 tsp. of ground nutmeg
- 2 tbsp. of ham
- Black pepper and salt
- 3 tbsp. of bread crumbs

Step-by-Step Directions to Cook It:

1. Mix pepper, nutmeg, leek, salt, beef, bread crumbs, and ham in a bowl. Scoop into small patties.
2. Transfer it to the basket that fits the air fryer. Cook for about 8 minutes at 400^{0}F.
3. Serve immediately as an appetizer.

Nutritional value per serving:

Calories: 255kcal, Fat: 11g, Carb: 0.8g, Proteins: 16g

Cheese Sticks

Perfect comfort food for days when you crave for sweet, delicious snacks.
Prep time and cooking time: 1 hour 20 minutes| Serves: 15

Ingredients To Use:

- 1 cup of grated parmesan
- 2 eggs
- 1 minced clove of garlic
- Black pepper and salt
- 1 tbsp. of Italian seasoning
- 8 strings of mozzarella cheese
- Cooking spray

Step-by-Step Directions to Cook It:

1. Mix pepper, garlic, salt, parmesan, and Italian seasoning in a bowl.
2. In another bowl, put the egg and whisk.
3. Put mozzarella in the egg mixture. Transfer to the cheese mixture. Put it inside egg again and then parmesan mixture. Put them in the refrigerator for about 1 hour.
4. Drizzle the cheese sticks with cooking spray. Transfer it to the air fryer. Cook for about 8 minutes at 390^0F.
5. Serve immediately as an appetizer.

Nutritional value per serving:

Calories: 400kcal, Fat: 35g, Carb: 2g, Proteins: 26g

Bacon Snack

Bacon in a meal is great but it is even greater as a snack.
Prep time and cooking time: 40 minutes| Serves: 16

Ingredients To Use:

- 1 tbsp. of avocado
- 1/2 tsp. of cinnamon powder
- 1 tsp. of maple extract
- 16 slices of bacon
- 3 ounces of avocado oil

Step-by-Step Directions to Cook It:

1. Put slices of bacon on the air fryer basket. Spray cinnamon powder on it. Cook for about 30 minutes at 300^0F.
2. Put oil inside a pot and heat over medium heat. Put chocolate and mix until the chocolate melts. Put maple extract. Remove the heat and allow it to cool down.
3. Put the bacon inside the chocolate mixture. Put it on a platter and allow it to cool down.
4. Serve when it is cold as a snack.

Nutritional value per serving:

Calories: 540kcal, Fat: 45g, Carb: 2g, Proteins: 40g

Chicken Rolls

You can enjoy these chicken rolls with a beer and some TV shows.
Prep time and cooking time: 2 hours 20 minutes| Serves: 12

Ingredients To Use:

- 2 chopped green onions
- Cooking spray
- 4 ounces of crumbled blue cheese
- 12 wrappers of egg roll
- 2 cups of cooked and chopped chicken
- 1/2 cup of tomato sauce
- Black pepper and salt
- 2 chopped celery stalks

Step-by-Step Directions to Cook It:

1. Mix pepper, tomato sauce, blue cheese, and celery in a bowl. Add chicken meat,

green onion, and salt.

2. Put the egg wrappers on a flat surface. Put the chicken mixture on it. Roll the wrapper and seal the edges.
3. Put the chicken rolls on the air fryer basket. Cook for about 10 minutes at 350°F.
4. Serve immediately as an appetizer.

Nutritional value per serving:

Calories: 260kcal, Fat: 6g, Carb: 40g, Proteins: 15g

Celery and Kale Crackers

This recipe creates an incredibly delicious snack.
Prep time and cooking time: 30 minutes|
Serves: 6

Ingredients To Use:

- 1 bunch of chopped basil
- 2 cups of ground flax seed
- 4 bunches of chopped kale
- 4 cloves of minced garlic
- 2 cups of overnight soaked flaxseed, drained
- 1/2 bunch of chopped celery
- 1/3 cup of olive oil

Step-by-Step Directions to Cook It:

1. Mix kale, garlic, celery, ground flaxseed, and celery in a food processor. Blend well.
2. Put soaked flaxseed and oil, then blend again. Pour the mixture on a pan that fits the air fryer.
3. Cook for about 20 minutes at 380°F.
4. Serve immediately as an appetizer.

Nutritional value per serving:

Calories: 145kcal, Fat: 5g, Carb: 7g, Proteins: 5g

Egg White chips

Egg white chips may seem weird at first, but you won't feel this way when you taste it's delicious crunchiness.
Prep time and cooking time: 15 minutes|
Serves: 2

Ingredients To Use:

- 4 egg whites
- 1/2 tbsp. of water
- Black pepper and salt
- 2 tbsp of shredded parmesan

Step-by-Step Directions to Cook It:

1. Mix pepper, egg whites, water, and salt in a bowl. Mix well.
2. Scoop the mixture into a muffin pan in the air fryer. Spray cheese on it. Cook for 8 minutes at 350°F.
3. Serve immediately as a snack.

Nutritional value per serving:

Calories: 50kcal, Fat: 0.3g, Carb: 0.8g, Proteins: 12g

Tuna Cake

A cake infused with seafood flavor. It tastes just right.
Prep time and cooking time: 20 minutes|
Serves: 12

Ingredients To Use:

- 1 tsp. of garlic powder
- 15 ounces of canned tuna
- 1/2 tsp. of dried dill
- Black pepper and salt
- 1/2 cup of chopped red onion
- Cooking spray
- 3 eggs
- 1 tsp. of dried parsley

Step-by-Step Directions to Cook It:

1. Mix pepper, parsley, eggs, and onion in a

bowl. Add dill, salt, garlic, and tuna. Make a medium cake shape out of it.
2. Put the tuna in the basket that fits the air fryer. Drizzle with cooking spray. Cook for 10 minutes at 350°F.
3. Serve immediately as an appetizer.

Shrimp and Calamari Snack

Get a slice of the sea with this seafood combination recipe.
Prep time and cooking time: 30 minutes|
Serves: 2

Ingredients To Use:

- 1 tsp. of tomato paste
- 8 ounces of calamari
- 1 tsp. of lemon juice
- 2 tbsp. of chopped avocado
- 7 ounces of deveined shrimps
- 1tbsp of olive oil
- ½ tsp. of turmeric powder
- Worcestershire sauce
- 1 tbsp. of mayonnaise
- Black pepper and salt
- 3 tbsp. of white flour
- 1 egg

Step-by-Step Directions to Cook It:

1. Put oil and egg in a bowl and whisk. Add shrimps and calamari rings.
2. Get another bowl, put pepper, flour, turmeric, and salt. Stir well.
3. Put shrimps and calamari in the flour mixture. Transfer it to the air fryer basket. Cook for about 9 minutes at 350°F.
4. Get another bowl, put mayonnaise, tomato paste, and avocado. Use a fork to mash well. Add lemon juice, pepper, Worcestershire sauce, and pepper. Stir well.
5. Serve shrimps and calamari with sauce.

Chapter 9: Dessert Recipes

Ginger Cheesecake

Ginger is a powerful medicinal plant that can be used as a spice. This Ginger cheesecake recipe contains ginger spice and cream cheese.

Prep time and cooking time: 2 hours 30 minutes| Serves: 7

Ingredients To Use:

- 1 tsp. of run
- 2 eggs
- 16 ounces of cream cookies
- 2 tsp. of butter
- 1/2 tsp. of vanilla extract
- 1/2 cup of sugar
- 1/2 cup of ginger cookies
- 1/2 tsp. of nutmeg

Step-by-Step Directions to Cook It:

1. Spread butter on a pan. Place cookies on the pan.
2. Mix nutmeg, rum, cream cheese, eggs, and vanilla in a bowl. Spread the mixture over the cookies.
3. Set the air fryer to a temperature of 340^0F. Cook for 20 minutes.
4. Allow the cheesecake to cool for about 2 hours.

Nutritional value per serving:

Calories: 415kcal, Fat: 13g, Carb: 22g, Proteins: 7g

Strawberry Pie

Strawberry pie is an excellent traditional dessert. The gelatine makes the flavor lasting and improves the taste.

Prep time and cooking time: 30 minutes|

Serves: 12

Ingredients To Use:

- 1 tsp. of gelatin
- 2 tbsp. of water
- 1/4 tsp. of stevia
- 1 cup of coconut oil
- 12 ounces of strawberries
- 1/2 tbsp. of lemon juice
- 1/4 cup of butter
- 1 cup of sunflower seeds
- 8 ounces of cream cheese
- 1/2 cup of heavy cream

Step-by-Step Directions to Cook It:

1. Mix butter, a pinch of salt, sunflower seeds, coconut in a food processor. Transfer it to a pan that fits the air fryer.
2. Put water in a pan and heat over medium heat. Put in gelatine and stir till the gelatine dissolves. Allow it to cool down.
3. Add the mixture to the food processor. Add lemon juice, 4 ounces of strawberries, stevia, and cream cheese and blend.
4. Put in heavy cream and stir. Spread the mixture over the crust. Put 8 ounces of strawberries on it.
5. Set the air fryer to 330^0F, cook for 15 minutes.
6. Serve immediately or leave to cool.

Nutritional value per serving:

Calories: 235kcal, Fat: 25g, Carb: 7g, Proteins: 8g

Coffee Cheesecakes

Coffee powder is gotten from the coffee

bean and has a lot of nutritional benefits. It is also the main ingredient of this amazing dessert. Try it out now, and you will not be disappointed.

Prep time and cooking time: 30 minutes| Serves: 6

Ingredients To Use:

- 4 tbsp. of caramel syrup
- 3 tbsp. of coffee
- 8 ounces of mascarpone cheese
- 8 ounces of cream cheese
- 1/3 cup of sugar
- 3 tbsp. of butter
- 2 Tbsp. of sugar
- 3 eggs

Step-by-Step Directions to Cook It:

1. Put 2 tbsp. of butter, 1/3 cup of sugar, and eggs in a blender. Add in 1 tbsp. of caramel syrup, cream cheese, and coffee. Pour the mixture into the cupcakes pan on the air fryer.
2. Set the air fryer at a temperature of 320°F, bake for about 20 minutes.
3. Mix 2 tbsp. of sugar, 3 tbsp. of butter, mascarpone in a bowl. Add in 3 tbsp. of caramel syrup. Blend the mixture well. Top the mixture on the cake and serve.

Nutritional value per serving:

Calories: 255kcal, Fat: 24g, Carb: 22g, Proteins: 6g

Cocoa Cookies

Who doesn't love cocoa cookies? They're perfect comfort foods and are always there for you when things get rough.

Prep time and cooking time: 25 minutes| Serves: 12

Ingredients To Use:

- 6 eggs
- 2 tsp. of vanilla

- 4 ounces of cream cheese
- 6 ounces of coconut oil
- 3 ounces of cocoa powder
- 5 tbsp. of sugar
- 1/2 tsp. of baking powder

Step-by-Step Directions to Cook It:

1. Pour the cocoa powder, vanilla, and coconut oil into a blender. Add eggs, cream cheese, and baking powder. Mix thoroughly.
2. Transfer the mixture to a baking dish that fits the air fryer. Set the temperature to 320°F, leave to bake for about 14-15 minutes.
3. Serve cookies immediately.

Nutritional value per serving:

Calories: 180kcal, Fat: 15g, Carb: 4g, Proteins: 6g

Special Brownies

The taste of this special brownie recipe is intensified by the walnut and peanut butter. Prep time and cooking time: 30 minutes| Serves: 4

Ingredients To Use:

- 1 tbsp. of peanut butter
- 7 tbsp. of butter
- 1/4 cup of chopped walnut
- 1/3 cup of cocoa powder
- 1/2 tsp. of baking powder
- 1/3 cup of sugar
- 1/4 cup of white flour
- 1/2 tsp. of vanilla extract
- 1 egg

Step-by-Step Directions to Cook It:

1. Add 6 tbsp. of butter to a medium pan placed over medium heat. Add sugar and stir. Cook for 5 minutes. Put the mixture in a bowl, add egg, walnut, vanilla extract, and salt. Add cocoa powder, flour, and

stir. Return the mixture to the pan that fits the air fryer.
2. Get another bowl, mix peanut butter, and 1 tbsp. of butter. Heat the mixture in the microwave for some seconds. Line it over the brownies.
3. Set the air fryer to a temperature of 320^{0}F, bake the brownies for about 18 minutes.
4. Allow cooling before serving.

Calories: 225kcal, Fat: 33g, Carb: 4g, Proteins: 7g

Blueberry Scones

Succulent blueberry scones are wonderful deserts. It is also a rare desert because of the dearth of blueberry.
Prep time and cooking time: 20 minutes| Serves: 10

Ingredients To Use:
- 1 cup of blueberries
- 1/2 cup of butter
- 2 tbsp. of vanilla extract
- 2 eggs
- 2 tbsp. of baking powder
- 1 cup of flour
- 5 tbsp. of sugar
- 1/2 cup of heavy cream

Step-by-Step Directions to Cook It:
1. Mix baking powder, flour, blueberries, and salt in a bowl.
2. Get another bowl, put vanilla extract, eggs, heavy cream, sugar, and butter. Mix well.
3. Transfer the 2 mixtures into another bowl and mix until it forms a dough. Cut the dough into 10 pieces in triangle shapes. Line them on the pan that fits the air fryer.

4. Set the air fryer to a temperature of 320^{0}F. Cook for 10 minutes.
5. Serve when it is cool.

Calories: 134kcal, Fat: 3g, Carb: 5g, Proteins: 4g

Chocolate Cookies

The is just the kind of cookie you want on a boring day to spice up your mood.
Prep time and cooking time: 35 minutes| Serves: 12

Ingredients To Use:
- 1 egg
- 2 cups of flour
- 1 tsp. of vanilla extract
- 1/2 cup of chocolate chips, unsweetened
- 1/2 cup of butter
- 4 tbsp. of sugar

Step-by-Step Directions to Cook It:
1. Put butter in a pan and heat over medium heat. Cook for about 1 minute.
2. Mix sugar, egg, and vanilla extract in a bowl.
3. Add half of the unsweetened chocolate chips and flour to the melted butter, stir well. Add the 2 mixtures together.
4. Pour the mixture on the pan that fits the air fryer. Put the remaining half of the chocolate chips.
5. Set the air fryer temperature at 330^{0}F, leave to bake for about 25 minutes.
6. Serve when cool.

Calories: 490kcal, Fat: 30g, Carb: 60g, Proteins: 8g

Tasty Orange Cake

This dessert is sweet, delicious, and healthy.

Prep time and cooking time: 43 minutes|
Serves: 13

Ingredients To Use:

- 1 tsp. of vanilla extract
- 2 ounces + 2 tbsp. of sugar
- 1 tsp. of baking powder
- 2 tbsp. of orange zest
- 4 ounces of yogurt
- 9 ounces of flour
- 1 orange
- 6 eggs
- 4 ounces of cream cheese

Step-by-Step Directions to Cook It:

1. Put the orange in a food processor and pulse until well-combined.
2. Add eggs, vanilla extract, flour, baking powder, and 2 tbsp of sugar. And pulse.
3. Place the mixture into spring pans that fit the air fryer. Set the air fryer to a temperature of 330^0F. Cook for about 15 minutes.
4. Get a bowl, mix yogurt, orange zest, and cream cheese. Add the remaining sugar and stir.
5. Put one layer of the cake on a plate. Put half of the cream cheese mixture. Put another layer of cake on it, pour the remaining cream cheese on it.
6. Serve immediately.

Nutritional value per serving:
Calories: 201kcal, Fat: 15g, Carb: 10g, Proteins: 9g

Macaroons

Macaroons are small cakes or cookies made from coconut or almond; they can also be made from any kind of nuts.
Prep time and cooking time: 20 minutes|
Serves: 20

Ingredients To Use:

- 1 tsp. of vanilla extract
- 4 egg whites
- 2 tbsp. of sugar
- 2 cups of shredded coconut

Step-by-Step Directions to Cook It:

1. Use a mixer to whisk stevia and egg whites.
2. Add vanilla extract with coconut. Whisk with mixer. Shape the mixture into a small ball in 20 pieces, put it in your pan that fit your air fryer. Set the air fryer to 340^0F. Cook for 9 minutes.
3. Serve when cold.

Nutritional value per serving:
Calories: 56kcal, Fat: 7g, Carb: 3g, Proteins: 2g

Lime Cheesecake

Lime is a fruit with a sour taste; though it is acidic, it has many nutritional benefits. Lime gives the meal a lasting flavor.
Prep time and cooking time: 4 hours 15 minutes| Serves: 10

Ingredients To Use:

- 1 pound of cream cheese
- 2 tbsp. of butter
- 1 lime zest
- 2 tsp. of sugar
- 2 cups of hot water
- 4 ounces of flour
- 2 sachets of lime jelly
- 1/4 cup of shredded coconut
- 1 lime juice

Step-by-Step Directions to Cook It:

1. Mix the butter, flour, sugar, and coconut in a bowl. Stir and transfer it to the pan that fits the air fryer.
2. Get another bowl, pour hot water and jelly sachets in it. Mix until the jelly sachet dissolves.

3. Add lime zest, cream cheese, and lime juice to the mixture. Pour the mixture on the crust in the pan.
4. Set air fryer to 300^{0}F. Cook for 5 minutes.
5. Allow cooling for about 4 hours.

Nutritional value per serving:

Calories: 262kcal, Fat: 24g, Carb: 6g, Proteins: 8g

Easy Granola

Granola can be served as a breakfast or a dessert.
Prep time and cooking time: 45 minutes| Serves: 4

Ingredients To Use:

- 1 tsp. of ground nutmeg
- 2 tbsp. of sugar
- 1/2 cup of almonds
- 2 tbsp. of sunflower oil
- 1 cup of shredded coconut
- 1/2 cup of pumpkin seed
- 1 tsp. of apple pie spice
- 1/2 cup of chopped pecan
- 1/2 cup of sunflower seeds

Step-by-Step Directions to Cook It:

1. Mix sunflower seeds, pecans, nutmeg, and almond in a bowl. Add in pumpkin seeds and apple pie spice, stir thoroughly.
2. Put oil in a pan and heat over medium heat. Put sugar and mix. Pour it on the coconut mixture. Stir.
3. Pour the mixture on a baking dish that fits the air fryer. Set the air fryer to 300°F. Bake for about 20-25 minutes.
4. Serve when cool.

Nutritional value per serving:

Calories: 325kcal, Fat: 8g, Carb: 14g, Proteins: 8g

Strawberry Cobbler

Cobbler is a dessert that contains different kinds of fruits. It is mostly baked but not fried.
Prep time and cooking time:35 minutes| Serves: 6

Ingredients To Use:

- 1 tbsp. of lemon juice
- 6 cups of halved strawberries
- A pinch of baking soda
- 3/4 cup of sugar
- 1/8 tsp. of baking powder
- 3-1/2 tbsp. of olive oil
- Cooking spray
- 1/2 cup of water
- 1/2 cup of flour

Step-by-Step Directions to Cook It:

1. Mix half of the sugar, lemon juice, and strawberries. Sprinkle flour, mix well. Pour the mixture on a greased baking sheet that fits the air fryer with cooking spray.
2. Get another bowl, put in baking powder, soda and sugar. Add in olive oil and mix. Put 1/2 cup of water. Spread the mixture over the strawberries.
3. Set the air fryer to 355^{0}F, leave to bake for 25 minutes.
4. Set the cobbler down and let it cool before serving.

Nutritional value per serving:

Calories: 222kcal, Fat: 4g, Carb: 8g, Proteins: 10g

Black Tea Cake

The black tea cake is produced by adding black tea to the ingredients of a yellow pound cake. It is a wonderful dessert.

Prep time and cooking time: 45 minutes|
Serves: 12

Ingredients To Use:

- 1 tsp. of baking soda
- 2 cups of milk
- 6 cups of sugar
- 4 eggs
- 1-1/2 cups of butter
- 6 tbsp. of black tea powder
- 3-1/2 cups of flour
- 2 tsp. of vanilla extract
- 6 tbsp. of honey
- 1/2 cup of olive oil
- 3 tsp. of baking powder

Step-by-Step Directions to Cook It:

1. Heat the milk over medium heat. Put in tea and stir. Stop the heat and leave to cool.
2. Mix 2 cups of sugar, vanilla extract, baking soda, and 1/2 cup of butter in a bowl. Add in eggs, baking powder, 1/2 cups of flour, and vegetable oil. Mix well.
3. Transfer the mixture to a greased pan that fits the air fryer. Set the air fryer to 330⁰F, bake for 20-25 minutes.
4. Mix 4 cups of sugar, 1 cup of butter, and honey in another bowl. Stir well.
5. Place the cake on a dish, pour cream over it, place another cake over it. Allow to cool down before serving.

Nutritional value per serving:

Calories: 201kcal, Fat: 5g, Carb: 7g, Proteins: 3g

Plum Cake

Plum cake is prepared by mixing dried fruit with cake ingredients. It is generally called fruit cake.
Prep time and cooking time: 2 hours | Serves: 8

Ingredients To Use:

- 1 ounce of butter
- 1 ounce of almond cake
- 5 tbsp. of sugar
- 7 ounces of flour
- 1 grated lemon zest
- 1 dried yeast
- 1-3/4 pounds of pitted plum
- 3 ounces of warm milk

Step-by-Step Directions to Cook It:

1. Mix 3 tbsp. of sugar, butter, and flour in a bowl. Add egg with milk, mix well until it forms a dough.
2. Place the dough on a butter greased spring pan that fits the air fryer. Cover it and leave for about 1 hour.
3. Sprinkle sugar on the plums. Transfer the pan to the air fryer and set it to 350⁰F. Leave to bake for 35 minutes.
4. Allow cooling before serving. Spray almond flakes on it and top with lemon zest.

Nutritional value per serving:

Calories: 195kcal, Fat: 5g, Carb: 8g, Proteins: 9g

Lentils Cookies

Lentils are edible legumes. They contains high protein and can also be called fiber powerhouse.
Prep time and cooking time: 35 minutes|
Serves: 30

Ingredients To Use:

- 1 cup of white flour
- 1 cup of butter
- 1 cup of raisins
- 1 cup of canned lentils
- 1 tsp. of baking powder
- 1 cup of shredded coconut
- 1/2 cup of brown sugar

- 1 cup of rolled oat
- 1 tsp. of cinnamon powder
- 1 egg
- 1 cup of whole wheat flour
- 2 tsp. of almond extract
- 1/2 cup of white sugar
- 1/2 tsp. of ground nutmeg
- 1 cup of water

Step-by-Step Directions to Cook It:

1. Mix the cinnamon, white flour, and baking powder in a bowl. Add whole wheat flour, nutmeg, and salt. Stir well.
2. Get another bowl, mix brown sugar, and white sugar. Whisk using kitchen mixer for about 2 minutes.
3. Add in lentil mix, oats, coconut, egg, flour mix, almond extract, raisins, and stir.
4. Use a tablespoon to scoop part of the dough and line it on the baking dish that fits the air fryer. Set the air fryer to 350^0F, bake for 15 minutes.
5. Serve immediately.

Nutritional value per serving:

Calories: 155kcal, Fat: 3g, Carb: 4g, Proteins: 10g

Lentils and Dates Brownies

This is an incredible dessert. The honey gives the brownies an awesome feel and also makes the flavor lasting.
Prep time and cooking time: 25 minutes | Serves: 8

Ingredients To Use:
- 1 tbsp. of honey
- 4 tbsp. of almond butter
- 12 dates
- 2 tbsp. of cocoa powder
- 28 ounces of canned lentils
- 1 chopped banana

- 4 tbsp. of almond butter
- 1/2 tsp. of baking soda

Step-by-Step Directions to Cook It:

1. Mix banana, baking soda, butter, honey, lentils in a food processor. Blend well.
2. Add the dates to the processor and continue blending. Transfer the mixture to a greased pan that fits the air fryer.
3. Set the air fryer to a temperature of 360^0F. Bake for 16 minutes.
4. Cut the brownies and serve.

Nutritional value per serving:

Calories: 163kcal, Fat: 5g, Carb: 4g, Proteins: 5g

Maple Cupcake

The flavor of maple syrup gives the cake a great taste. Adequately whisked Butter and eggs also make the cake fluffy.
Prep time and cooking time: 30 minutes | Serves: 4

Ingredients To Use:
- 1 tsp. of vanilla extract
- 1/2 tsp. of baking powder
- 1/2 cup of pure applesauce
- 4 tsp. of maple syrup
- 1/2 chopped apple
- 2 tsp. of cinnamon powder
- 3/4 cup of white flour
- 4 eggs
- 4 tbsp. of butter

Step-by-Step Directions to Cook It:

1. Put butter in a pan and heat over medium heat. Add eggs, applesauce, maple syrup, and vanilla. Whisk well. Remove the heat and allow it to coOl.
2. Add in baking powder, flour, apples, and cinnamon. Mix well.
3. Transfer the mixture to a cupcake pan

that fits the air fryer. Set the air fryer at 350°F. Bake for about 15-20 minutes.

4. Serve immediately or allow to cool down.

Nutritional value per serving:
Calories: 165kcal, Fat: 5g, Carb: 4g, Proteins: 5g

Rhubarb Pie

Rhubarb pie may have extra sugar than appropriate, but the calories are definitely worth it.

Prep time and cooking time: 1 hour 15 minutes | Serves: 6

Ingredients To Use:

- 9 tbsp. of butter
- 3 cups of chopped rhubarb
- 1/2 tsp. of nutmeg
- 2-1/2 cups of sugar
- 2 tbsp. of low-fat milk
- 5 tbsp. of cold water
- 3 tbsp. of flour
- 1-1/2 cups of almond flour
- 2 eggs

Step-by-Step Directions to Cook It:

1. Mix cold water, 1 tsp. of sugar, 1-1/4 cup of flour, and 8 tbsp. of butter in a bowl. Mix until it forms a dough.
2. Put the dough on a floured flat surface and cut. Put inside the fridge and allow it to stay for about 30 minutes. Bring it out and place it in a pie pan that suits the air fryer.
3. In another bowl, mix 3 tbsp. of flour, 1-1/2 cups of sugar, rhubarb, and nutmeg. Mix well.
4. Get another bowl, put milk, and egg. Whisk well. Put it inside the rhubarb mix. Pour all the mixture into the pie crust. Set the air fryer to 390°F. Bake for about 45 minutes.
5. Serve when cold.

Nutritional value per serving:
Calories: 201kcal, Fat: 3g, Carb: 7g, Proteins: 4g

Lemon Tart

This lemon tart recipe contains lemon zest and lemon juice.

Prep time and cooking time: 1 hour 40 minutes| Serves: 6

Ingredients To Use:

- 12 tbsp. of cold butter
- 2 lemon zest
- 2 tbsp. and 1-1/4 cups of sugar
- 10 tbsp. of chilled, melted butter
- 2 cups of white flour
- 2 lemon juice
- 3 tbsp. of ice water
- 2 eggs
- Salt, a pinch

Step-by-Step Directions to Cook It:

1. Mix 2 tbsp. of sugar, 2 cups of white flour, and salt in a bowl. Whisk well.
2. Add water and 12 tbsp. of butter. Mix until it forms a dough. Give it a ball shape and wrap it in a foil. Leave in the refrigerator for 1 hour.
3. Put the dough on a floured flat surface. Transfer it to a tart pan that fits the air fryer. Set to 350°F, bake for 16 minutes.
4. Get another bowl, put 10 tbsp of butter, lemon zest, 1-1/4 cup of sugar, lemon juice, and eggs. Whisk well.
5. Pour the mixture on the pie crust. Set the air fryer to 360°F temperature. Cook for 19 minutes.
6. Serve immediately.

Nutritional value per serving:
Calories: 185kcal, Fat: 5g, Carb: 3g, Proteins: 5g

Mandarin Pudding

Mandarin is a tiny fruit that originates from China. It is readily available in local grocery stores.

Prep time and cooking time: 60 minutes | Serves: 8

- 2 eggs
- 2 mandarins juice
- 3/4 cup of sugar
- 1 peeled, sliced mandarin
- 3/4 cup of ground almond
- 2 tbsp. of brown sugar
- Honey
- 4 ounces of soft butter
- 3/4 cup of white flour

Step-by-Step Directions to Cook It:

1. Put the butter in a pan, put slices of mandarin in it and sprinkle with brown sugar.
2. Mix eggs, almond, mandarin juice, and sugar in a bowl. Add flour and stir. Pour the mixture on the mandarin slices. Put the pan in the air fryer. Set the air fryer to 360^0F temperature. Cook for 35-40 minutes.
3. Serve immediately and top with honey.

Nutritional value per serving:

Calories: 165kcal, Fat: 5g, Carb: 5g, Proteins: 8g

Strawberry Shortcake

Shortcake is a crumbly sweet biscuit or cake that's crunchier than shortbread. It is less dense; it has contains more carbonhydrate.

Prep time and cooking time: 65 minutes | Serves: 7

Ingredients To Use:

- 1 tbsp. of rum
- 1-1/2 cups of flour
- 1/2 cup of whipping cream
- 1/4 cup of sugar and 4 tbsps.
- 1 tsp. of grated lime zest
- 1/3 cup of butter
- 1 egg
- 1 tbsp. of chopped mint
- 1 tsp. of baking powder
- 2 cups of strawberries
- 1 cup of buttermilk
- 1/4 tsp. of baking soda
- Cooking spray

Step-by-Step Directions to Cook It:

1. Mix the baking powder, flour, baking soda, and 1/4 cup of sugar in a bowl and stir.
2. Get another bowl, mix egg, flour mix, and buttermilk. Whisk well.
3. Shape the dough into 6 greased jar with cooking spray. Place foil on it. Transfer it to the air fryer and cook for 45 minutes at 360^0F.
4. In a bowl, put in rum, strawberries, lime zest, 3 tbsp. of sugar, and mint. Mix well and leave in a cold place.
5. Get another bowl, put 1 tbsp. of sugar, whipping cream, and stir.
6. Bring the jars out. Put on strawberry mix and top with whipped cream.

Nutritional value per serving:

Calories: 350kcal, Fat: 15g, Carb: 50g, Proteins: 8g

Sponge Cake

Sponge cake is also called a naked cake because it is not covered with icing sugar.

Prep time and cooking time: 30 minutes | Serves: 11

Ingredients To Use:

- 1 cup of olive oil

- 1-1/2 cup of milk
- 1-2/3 cup of sugar
- 3 cups of flour
- 2 tsp. of vanilla extract
- 3 tsp. of baking powder
- 1/4 cup of lemon juice
- 2 cups of water
- 1/2 cup of cornstarch
- 1 tsp. of baking soda

Step-by-Step Directions to Cook It:

1. Mix baking powder, sugar, flour, baking soda, and cornstarch in a bowl and whisk.
2. Get another bowl, mix vanilla, oil, water, lemon juice, and milk. Whisk well.
3. Mix the 2 mixtures. Transfer it to a greased baking dish that fits the air fryer. Set the air fryer at 350°F temperature. Bake for 20 minutes.
4. Allow cooling before serving.

Nutritional value per serving:

Calories: 300kcal, Fat: 5g, Carb: 60g, Proteins: 8g

Ricotta and Lemon Cake

Ricotta cake is a fluffy, rich cake with good density due to the great number of eggs used to make the cake.

Prep time and cooking time: 1 hour 20 minutes | Serves: 4

Ingredients To Use:

- 1 grated lemon zest
- 3 pounds of ricotta cheese
- Butter
- 1 grated orange zest
- 8 eggs
- 1/2 pound of sugar

Step-by-Step Directions to Cook It:

1. Mix the cheese, orange zest, eggs, lemon zest, and sugar in a bowl.

2. Put butter in the baking pan that fits the air fryer. Pour the mixture into the pan at bake at 390°F for 30 minutes.
3. Lower the air fryer heat to 380°F, leave to bake for another 40 minutes.
4. Bring out of the oven and allow to cool before serving.

Nutritional value per serving:

Calories: 113kcal, Fat: 5g, Carb: 5g, Proteins: 8g

Orange Cookies

It is no new thing that orange is a citrus fruit, and it is a good source of vitamin C. This recipe takes advantage of its dulcet taste to make a tropical snack.

Prep time and cooking time: 25 minutes | Serves: 8

Ingredients To Use:

- 1 tsp. off vanilla extract
- 4 ounces of cream cheese
- 1 tsp. of baking powder
- 2-3/4 cup of sugar
- 1 tbsp. of orange zest
- 2 cups of flour
- 1 cup of butter
- 1 egg

Step-by-Step Directions to Cook It:

1. Mix 1/2 cup of butter, cream cheese, and 2 cups of sugar in a bowl. Use a mixer to stir.
2. Get another bowl, put baking powder and flour, and mix.
3. Get the third bowl, mix egg, 3/4 cup of sugar, orange zest, 1/2 cup of butter, and vanilla extract. Mix well.
4. Combine the orange mixture and flour mixture in one bowl. Scoop the mixture with a tablespoon and put in a baking dish that fits the air fryer.

5. Do the same for the remaining orange batter. Set the air fryer to 340^0F, bake for 12 minutes.
6. Allow it to cool before serving. Top with cream fillings and serve.

Nutritional value per serving:

Calories: 156kcal, Fat: 14g, Carb: 21g, Proteins: 11g

Cashew Bars

Though cashew has a sour taste, it tastes incredible when used in this recipe to make cashew bars.

Prep time and cooking time: 25 minutes | Serves: 6

Ingredients To Use:

- 1 tbsp. of almond butter
- 3/4 cup of shredded coconut
- 1/3 cup of honey
- 1-1/2 cup of chopped cashews
- 4 chopped dates
- 1 tbsp. of chia seeds
- 1/4 cup of almond meal

Step-by-Step Directions to Cook It:

1. Mix almond butter, honey, and almond meal in a bowl and stir.
2. Add dates, cashew, chia seeds, and coconuts and stir well.
3. Pour the mixture on a baking dish that fits that air fryer.
4. Set the air fryer temperature to 300^0F. Bake for about 15 minutes.
5. Allow cooling before service.

Nutritional value per serving:

Calories: 122kcal, Fat: 7g, Carb: 9g, Proteins: 11g

Brown Butter Cookies

Brown butter is also called beurre noisette. It is gotten from cooking butter until it turns brown.

Prep time and cooking time: 20 minutes| Serves:

Ingredients To Use:

- 2 cups of brown sugar.
- 2 tsp. of vanilla extract
- 2/3 cup of chopped pecan
- 1-1/2 cups of butter
- 3 cups of flour
- 1/2 tsp. of baking powder
- 2 eggs
- 1 tsp. of baking soda

Step-by-Step Directions to Cook It:

1. Put butter in a pan and heat over medium heat. Put brown sugar and stir.
2. Get another bowl, mix vanilla extract, flour, eggs, baking soda, and pecans. Add baking powder and brown butter. Stir and scoop with a spoon and line it on the baking pan that suits the air fryer.
3. Set the air fryer to 340^0F, bake for 10 minutes.
4. Allow cookies to cool before serving.

Nutritional value per serving:

Calories: 150kcal, Fat: 7g, Carb: 10g, Proteins: 20g

Sweet Potato Cheesecake

Each cheesecake recipe has a secret ingredient that makes it unique. Cinnamon gives this recipe extra boost.

Prep time and cooking time: 15 minutes| Serves: 5

Ingredients To Use:

- 1 tsp. of vanilla extract
- 6 ounces of soft mascarpone
- 3/4 cup of milk
- 2/3 cup of sweet potato puree
- 8 ounces of soft cream cheese
- 1/4 tsp. of cinnamon powder

- 2/3 cup of crumbled graham crackers
- 4 tbsp. of melted butter

1. Mix the crumbled crackers and butter in a bowl. Pour it into a cake pan that suits the air fryer.
2. Get another bowl, mix sweet potato puree, cream cheese, and cinnamon. Add vanilla extract, mascarpone, and milk.
3. Pour the mixture on the crust. Set the air fryer to 300⁰F. Bake for 4 minutes.
4. Allow to cool down in the refrigerator before serving.

Nutritional value per serving:

Calories: 173kcal, Fat: 12g, Carb: 18g, Proteins: 15g

Peach Pie

Peach pie is a traditional pie that is prepared in a traditional home. It has always tasted great for generations and still tastes great.
Prep time and cooking time: 45 minutes|
Serves: 4

Ingredients To Use:
- 1 tbsp. of dark rum
- 1/2 cup of sugar
- 2 tbsp. of cornstarch
- Ground nutmeg, a pinch
- 2-1/4 pounds of chopped peaches
- 2 tbsp. of melted butter
- 1 pie dough
- 2 tbsp. of flour
- 1 tbsp. of lemon juice

Step-by-Step Directions to Cook It:

1. Put the pie dough into a pie pan that suits the air fryer.
2. Mix the sugar, nutmeg, cornstarch, rum, butter, peaches, and lemon juice in a bowl. Stir.
3. Pour the mixture into the pie pan. Set the air fryer at 350⁰F. Cook for 30-35 minutes.
4. Serve immediately or allow to cool.

Nutritional value per serving:

Calories: 230kcal, Fat: 10g, Carb: 15g, Proteins: 10g

Conclusion

There is no doubt that the Ultrean Air Fryer is an appliance that makes cooking more fun and easier than ever. Stop aimless searching and spending extra money on several appliances. The Ultrean Air Fryer will be a magic appliance in your kitchen!

We hope this guide has given you a better understanding of the instruction, the features, and the convenience in this appliance.

Manufactured by Amazon.ca
Bolton, ON

25660592R00061